A SONG FOR ALL SEASONS

Harmony in the Inner Life

MARION K. RICH

Foreword by
Alice Johnson

BEACON HILL PRESS OF KANSAS CITY
KANSAS CITY, MISSOURI

Lovingly dedicated to Louise—
my professor, confidante, and friend,
who believed in me, motivated me, and inspired me
always to do my best.

Contents

Foreword

Harmony in the inner life is the miraculous work of God's grace through conversion and the indwelling fullness of the Holy Spirit.

One quickly becomes aware of the seasons of life, not necessarily the "age" seasons, but those cited in Ecclesiastes 3, which begins, "There is a time for everything, and a season for every activity under heaven."

Marion beautifully weaves these truths into the tapestry of this book, as she expounds the joy of harmony in the inner life. This harmony should be the goal of every Christian, so that a melodious song might exude through one's entire personality.

Marion has served alongside her husband as pastor's wife, missionary, teacher in Haiti, and district superintendent's wife. She was the pioneer director and coordinator of Women in Leadership Conferences (WILCON I). She has penned numerous articles and several books. She is a sought-after speaker, a devoted mother, wife, and friend. Through the years, she has been deeply enveloped in the experiences of life but has always emerged with that glowing evidence of harmony within, which the Holy Spirit orchestrates in her life.

—ALICE JOHNSON

Preface

"What mankind needs is a song to sing and a creed to believe," remarked a former president of Harvard University. As long as Christ is the mainspring of that creed, then I agree—this is what we all need. The song will come spontaneously within our souls when our faith in Him is our personal, positive response to His character. Christ has a way of breaking through the maze of dogma, ritual, and creed with an immensely life-changing experience. He is the focal point of Christian faith. There comes to us an inner sense of well-being centered in that experience, and the music resounds within because we know whom we believe and what we believe. So just as the melodic song of birds soars up to meet the light on a warm spring morning, Christians who have opened their lives to Christ's gentle leading have a song in their soul for all seasons.

The earliest creed of the Christian church was, "Jesus Christ is Lord." He is the Master and Owner of all life, the One who changed history forever—the Christ of the eternities who gives us a sense of destiny and direction. He is the turning point of our lives. The essence of our creed has always been expressed through music—precisely the sort of vivid, infectious, poetic, and exciting music that speaks to the soul.

This is a book about our creed—what we believe—and about the song that comes from the inner harmony of a consecrated life. That inner harmony is translated into an outer harmony. Even in the circumstances of life where joy would seem to be impossible and there seems to be nothing but pain and discomfort, the Christian has an inner strength from an abiding joy in the Lord. Jesus told us it would be that way, "No one will take away your joy" (John 16:22).

A friend once asked the aged maestro Toscanini why he played so little contemporary music. He replied, "I am the man who did Wagner when Wagner was new, who produced all the moderns from Strauss and Debussy to Sibelius. Now let the other young men do what I did . . . I want, I crave the time in these my last years, to come a little nearer to the secrets of Beethoven and a very few other eternal masters."[1] I believe the divine Master Musician wants us to draw a little closer to Him that we may learn more of His secrets and allow Him to tune our imperfect human instruments. By His Spirit He will eliminate the discords and strident notes from our lives. His perfect attunement will result in a holy harmony.

The great cycle of the seasons will go on year after year, but His faithfulness will be our portion. And so we sing:

> *Summer and winter, and springtime and harvest,*
> *Sun, moon, and stars in their courses above,*
> *Join with all nature in manifold witness*
> *To Thy great faithfulness, mercy, and love.* *
>
> —THOMAS O. CHISHOLM

Acknowledgments

I owe a debt of gratitude to the many writers whose works I have read and whose spirit, insights, and impressions have no doubt become a part of my own thinking and writing. Every effort has been made to give credit wherever a source could be traced. Many of the reflections and quotations had been recorded in years past in my personal journals.

A special thanks to Sharon Harvey, my daughter, who wrote the segment on "Creative Ways to Praise God." She is one who has learned to live a life of praise.

To Harry, the finest companion a woman could have, I owe deep appreciation. He has helped to create the quiet spaces in my life by freeing me many times from the constant demands of work, travel, and household tasks. Without his constant love, encouragement, and support this work could not have been completed.

Then most of all, I am grateful to my living Lord, whose gracious presence has given me direction and guidance. To Him I owe my all and offer this book for His glory.

PART ONE

Prelude

1

Hearing the Music

As we walked swiftly through the busy airport concourse, my mind was whirling with thoughts of the theme of this book, *A Song for All Seasons*. Glancing at a huge billboard that caught my attention, the word *music* leaped out at me. I tried to read it quickly, then noticed that my husband's characteristic speed had taken him several paces ahead of me; and he was looking back to hasten me on.

"Why were you stopping?" he asked when I caught up with him.

"Because I wanted to read a quote about music on the billboard," I replied with a quickness in my voice. "But you wouldn't wait for me!"

After we were situated in the waiting area of our gate, he disappeared for a while. When he returned he handed me a piece of paper. He had returned to the concourse and copied the quote for me: "Music is written to take people's minds away from famine, plague, and pestilence and will make you forget about long lines, lost luggage, and that tinfoil-wrapped chicken thing."

We both laughed. "It really isn't what I had in mind," I said, "but thanks for going all the way back to copy it for me."

Later, I thought about the essence of the quote on the billboard. How true that our contemporary world tries to forget about the famine, plague, and pestilence. It does not want to think about human suffering, hunger, the destruction caused by the recent war, or even the small inconveniences of life—such as long lines or lost luggage. It wants distractions. "Forget about the cares and problems, the need of the world"—this is the attitude of many. Loud, raucous music is in style. It blares away in our ears more often than we'd like—in TV commercials, in public places, even when put on "hold" when using the telephone. How rare are the soft musical cadences of a melodious symphony or the rhythm of a classical piece or even the gentle strains of an old hymn.

Yesterday I sat in a dentist's office and even there I was surprised at the background music. First the wild beat of the drums, then the screeching singer, the syncopated rhythm, the swinging beat—all designed, no doubt, to produce a pleasant sensation for the listener. To me it was anything but conducive to relaxing in a dentist's chair.

Last week I walked into a store and the volume of the music was turned up so loud that I could feel the beat pounding in my head. I said to the sales clerk, "How can you stand to work here with the music so loud?"

She smiled and said, "Oh, that's the only thing that keeps me going."

It seems that many in today's world seek to satisfy their thirst for joy from a sensual source. To seek such gratification is to leave one's questing spirit unsatisfied and disillusioned. How true are the oft-quoted words of Augustine: "Thou hast formed us for thyself, and our hearts are restless till they find rest in Thee." A peace that comes from God is a quiet, potent attitude of serenity. By His Spirit He transmits to us His life, vitality, and enthusiasm. God alone is the Source and Supplier of the quality of life we long for in our everyday experiences.

Discriminating Ears

Christians can hear a different kind of music if we will listen carefully. It is not the kind of music that drowns out the things we do not like, nor the kind of music that makes us forget about distasteful circumstances. Rather, it is a song from the Spirit of God that reminds us of our Heavenly Father's constant presence. In fact, it may be a verse of Scripture, or even a recurring phrase that has gripped our minds that day. Despite the clamor of the crowds, the drone of aircraft, the insistence of the noises of the modern world, the song within that comes from Him can speak to our spirit in soft, clear tones.

To hear God speak to us we must develop a sense of discernment—discriminating ears, so to speak. It means developing a sensitivity to the Holy Spirit so that we can tune in to His voice. On one level we are doing the activities of the day, but on a deeper, more profound level, we are listening to God. Inwardly we can pray, praise, worship, and hear His song—a perpetual receptivity of spirit. Since we are involved in thinking that never ceases, we can think in dialogue with God. We can move from self-centered monologue to a conversation with God. The intimacy with the Lord that is privately disciplined will then be experienced in many nonprivate situations in the course of a day. By learning how to listen to God we learn to listen better to other people too.

The Listening Habit

I first heard about "the listening habit" from a college professor. It was her overall "help to holy living"—her way of responding to Christ's moment-by-moment, offered fellowship. Bertha Munro, the dean of Eastern Nazarene College for 40 years, and professor of literature, was one whose piety came with her into the classroom. She had the ability to communicate her philosophy of life to her students. One of the spiritual themes of her life is indelibly etched on my memory. She called it, "the listening habit"—listening for God to speak to her each day through song and Scripture.

"You know how it is," she would say. "A Bible verse or a

gospel song one day comes alive to you and is yours forever. For the first time words old or new will catch your mind and your imagination, and grip your heart."

She would often speak of God's own gift to her—His surprise of waking her every morning with a song.

We students sought to emulate her. Through the years I have made a conscious effort to cultivate the listening habit.

For me Christ's song does not always come at the moment of awakening—but it does come clearly in the morning as I begin to worship Him in the quiet place of my study. The song comes to me, and it usually stays with me throughout the day. It may be a song I have not heard in years or one that was sung in church on Sunday. There are times I read the words to several songs in my hymnal and one seems to stay. I know it is the Holy Spirit who makes this listening habit the voice of God to me as I will to think and praise and obey.

Our Chatty Society

James tells us that everyone should be quick to listen and slow to speak. Luke in his Gospel admonishes us to consider carefully how we listen. Most of us are better at talking than at listening. Henri Nouwen writes, "One of our main problems is that in this chatty society, silence has become a very fearful thing. For most people silence creates itchiness and nervousness. Many experience silence not as full and rich but as empty and hollow. For them silence is like a gaping abyss which can swallow them up."[1]

In the book *Worship: Rediscovering the Missing Jewel,* authors Allen and Borror say that persons have no song to sing in our present society because of the pressures of life without purpose (without Christ), and because we are so surrounded by music in our cars, homes, and restaurants that we have no silence to fill with song.[2]

Failing to Hear the Warning

I am reminded of the night we watched the story on the news. The four elderly women were driving a new Chrysler sedately across the causeway bridge. Laughing and chatting gaily with each other, they failed to hear the bells warning that the bridge was to be raised. They were already past the first gate and on the metal-grated drawspan before they saw the gates come down. The bridge tender thought the bridge was clear of traffic. He was watching an approaching yacht whose tall mast was the reason for raising the bridge.

As the drawspan rose slowly, the four women realized they were going up with it. The front wheels of the car were on, the back wheels off the drawspan. They froze in their seats afraid to move for fear of upsetting the balance of the car.

When the bridge tender looked up he could hardly believe what he saw. There was the car just hanging. He stopped the bridge, but by this time the women were perched 50 feet above the island waterway, at a 45-degree angle. He phoned for help and watched the car apprehensively. He wondered how they could have missed hearing the signals and wondered how long their car would stay balanced up there.

The four women were praying for help. They sat as motionless as possible, afraid the least movement would send them crashing down into the water.

Below them, sailboats, motorboats, and cabin cruisers gathered in the water. Within minutes firemen and policemen answered the call for help.

First, they put a long ladder on the drawspan, and several firemen crawled up to the car. They tried to keep the ladies calm. The car was still running and one of the fireman reached in and turned off the ignition. Next they fastened the car to the bridge grates with bolts and cables. Finally, they brought a big snorkel truck and lifted them down. A fireman held them close as one by one they inched their way to the snorkel and were safely lowered to the ground. They were wrapped in warm blankets and rushed by ambulance to the hospital for observation.

Many praised the elderly women for their courage during the two hour ordeal. These ladies did not deliberately ignore the bells and warning lights. They were just busy talking and neglected to watch and listen.

What about us? Sometimes I wonder how often Christians ignore the voice of God when He tries to speak and alert us to the danger of spiritual decline in our personal lives. Many times we get busy and fail to come before the Lord long enough to hear Him.

The Book of Habakkuk is an interesting and instructive one in the Bible. In the first chapter the prophet is dismayed and perplexed and argues with the Lord. He complains about the lack of justice in God's management of the world. But in the second chapter he says, "I will stand at my watch and . . . see what [the Lord] will say to me" (v. 1). Listening to God is part of the transaction of relationship with Him.

The songwriter wrote:

> *Open my ears, that I may hear*
> *Voices of truth Thou sendest clear;*
> *And while the wave-notes fall on my ear,*
> *Ev'rything false will disappear.*
> —Clara H. Scott

PART TWO

Major Chords

2

The Keynote of Grace

There is something tremendously solemn and decisive about the choice one makes in accepting or rejecting Christ. The gospel message of the New Testament is the only message that promises divine help to humankind in their sins. It is a message that calls us out of our sins entirely.

I can remember when the song "Amazing Grace, How Sweet the Sound" became popular and was one of the best-sellers in rock music. It was not by chance that the song was loved—for God's grace has an affinity with human beings and with human desire. Transforming grace can be seen around the world wherever people come to Jesus Christ as He awakens their personality and sets them free from the guilt of sin.

I recall an incident that meant much to me while serving as a missionary to Haiti. Sitting beneath a large shade tree, I was visiting with Madame Jacques, a leading Christian in the community where we had been holding services. The aroma of fresh, strong Haitian coffee filled the air as we talked together.

"There is a man who is responsible for killing hundreds of people in our village, including my grandmother," she stated emphatically, her dark eyes watching me intently.

Noting the look of alarm on my face, she continued.

"We have experienced a great victory in our community. Christ has shattered the hold of Satan on a voodoo priest."

Slowly Madame Jacques poured the black, aromatic coffee into tiny cups and resumed her conversation. She began to explain the awesome power of a voodoo priest in her culture. Her descriptions were incredible as she reached into her primitive past and blended it with the present. I listened avidly. No wonder so many people had been getting converted in this voodoo-steeped village, I thought. Since leaders in voodoo were accepting Christ in this area, others felt they could come to Him without great fear.

As she talked I could still picture the four young people who came running to our mission station a few weeks before. Their speech brimmed with excitement.

"He has decided to get converted," they cried, all of them chattering simultaneously in Creole.

Trying to sort out their animated words I asked, "Who wants to get converted?"

"Mr. Pierre, the voodoo priest in the village of Fragneau," one repeated breathlessly.

As a result two single missionary women and I set out in the mission van. The Jeep was already being used by the missionary men who had gone to the interior that week. We arrived in the village, left the van at the bottom of a steep hill, and set off in a single file up a rocky path toward Mr. Pierre's house. There was an ominous and constant thundering, and we were aware of the play of lightning like bright signals from hill to hill. We moved very briskly before the storm could burst.

By the time we reached the tin-covered Haitian house the rain was beginning to fall. Mr. and Mrs. Pierre greeted us warmly. A small lamp on the table flickered uncertainly, and we could smell the burning diesel fuel.

Mr. Pierre was a tall, stately gentleman with white hair and mustache. He looked very dignified. His wife was small and unassuming—probably much younger than he. However, she was thought of as a powerful voodoo priestess in the community. Just two weeks before, Madame Pierre was converted while her husband was out of town. At her conversion she had us burn valuable voodoo charms and break the bottles of bad-smelling solutions filled with so-called remedies to keep away evil spirits. The radical change in her life and her glowing witness to her husband made Mr. Pierre hungry for the same peace that his wife was enjoying. Tonight he had made his decision. He needed to make his peace with God.

We read some verses from God's Word and explained the plan of salvation—that Christ is the mighty power of God to save us and that He himself is the center of God's wise plan of salvation. We spoke of the Cross, the love of God, and emphasized the cost of discipleship. Mr. Pierre kept nodding and declaring, "I have made up my mind. I want to accept Christ!" He understood what it involved.

When we knelt to pray, that homely little room was transformed by the Shechinah glory. It was a momentous evening. We could almost hear the scratch of the recording angel's pen as he wrote a new name in the Lamb's Book of Life. The little tin lamp continued to burn and smoke, and great, whirling sheets of rain swept down noisily against the tin roof. But a glow and radiance filled the room as Mr. Pierre drew his wife close and said, "Cheri, we're going to walk this way together now." He turned toward us and testified, "Drink and tobacco have been killing me, Satan has been eating me, but now Christ has changed me."

The storm that had raged within the heart of this voodoo priest had now subsided. Outside the house the storm was also gone. As we left the little Haitian house with our hearts overflowing with praise, a great fragrance arose from the refreshed and watered earth, the fragrance of eternal, pulsing life. The night was cool and clear. A steel-white moon was beginning to cast a sheen of brilliant glory across the heavens. There was something about a night like this that filled me with confidence in the people and the land.

It is possible for any person to come to know Christ. No sin is too great for Him to wash away. The new life of the risen Christ sets the spirit free. Jesus himself said so, "If the Son sets you free, you will be free indeed" (John 8:36). Once again the miracle—the miracle of God veritably present where it seemed no God could possibly be—redeeming, reconciling, justifying, transforming, assuring. What a God is He! It is no wonder the Psalmist declared: "He has given me a new song to sing, of praises to our God. Now many will hear of the glorious things he did for me, and stand in awe before the Lord, and put their trust in him" (Ps. 40:3, TLB).

Mr. Pierre was now free to follow Christ, free from the darkness and superstitions that bound him, free from the fear of evil spirits, free from the guilt of sin. He would walk regularly three miles to the mission chapel to pray early in the mornings. He was filled with abundant energy and life in the Son of God—"who loved [him] and gave himself for [him]" (Gal. 2:20). This voodoo priest experienced Christ's triumphant, overcoming life by His presence and His resurrection power.

The message of the gospel stresses the need for total conversion—the need of becoming a new creature in Christ. Christianity is more than a moral reformation; it produces a radical transformation of the human heart. Its conditions are confession of sin, faith in Christ's atoning blood and in His resurrection, and obedience to Christ.

Genuine salvation really works and satisfies. It gives peace of mind, takes away the fear of death, saves from corrupting, degrading habits, and puts a new song in the heart. The heart of one who is genuinely saved from sin is in tune with God and spiritual verities. There is no willful, continuous practice of sin in such a life, but there is evidence of fruit. Redemption is the keynote of grace. One who has been redeemed by Christ has an authentic creed to believe and a joyous song to sing.

> 'Tis the song of the soul set free;
> And its melody is ringing.
> 'Tis the song of the soul set free;
> Joy and peace to me it's bringing.*
> —Oswald J. Smith

3

The Melody of Love

That morning Joanna stepped outside and found a world full of flashing sunlight and brilliant hues of color. Songs, glorious songs, were welling up from her heart, and she wanted to sing them from the top of her voice. "I sing for I cannot be silent," she exclaimed. God had met the deep need in her life.

For years she had struggled with sinful attitudes and emotional conflicts. A spirit of bitterness and unforgiveness kept welling up in her heart against her father who had abused her as a child and deserted the family in a time of crisis. Ever since she became a born-again Christian and had decided to follow Christ, she longed to be used of God and to live a life of victory. But the deep emotional scars continued to trouble her. And the memories of the past—the vicious, bruising battleground—became a source of defeat to her. As a result she would find herself reacting negatively, with resentment, toward others.

It was hard for Joanna to realize that in order to receive God's grace and forgiveness, it was important for her to give unconditional love and forgiveness to others. Not long ago in a revival service the Spirit of God revealed to Joanna the ugliness of her unforgiving spirit, the bitterness and the unkind reactions toward others. She began to fully realize that Jesus was a victim of unrequited love. He had been betrayed, even by those He loved, to the point of death.

Finally she came to a place where she sought God for a cleansing of her inward pollution. She allowed the forgiving, healing grace of God to come into all the memories that were keeping pain alive. Accepting Christ's total forgiveness for her resentments, she also expressed her forgiveness for the one who caused the pain. She explained that for her, the toughest petition in the Lord's Prayer had been, "Forgive us our [sins] as we forgive those who [sin] against us."

As she prayed and sought God's purifying power, Joanna felt an overwhelming sense of love. God's unutterable love poured forth into her heart with the new, energizing force of the Holy Spirit. Inwardly she was awakened to the light of a brand-new day. Her experience of God was heightened to a new dimension of understanding and experience. The fullness of God's Spirit had come to her from the role of prayer, to the emptying of herself, to an entire consecration of her being.

Today this young woman enjoys peace and contentment. The bitterness and restless agitation are gone. Her whole life is open to the love of God. Instead of her ego clamoring for first place she exhibits compassion, helpfulness, and understanding. Her life is being used by God as a channel to touch others.

This deeper spiritual experience of the Holy Spirit's fullness and cleansing power is not something unique to Joanna, but it is the same kind of spiritual encounter the disciples had on the day of Pentecost. It is needed very much by believers today and is available to them. Countless millions through the ages have recognized that holy living becomes possible by means of the Holy Spirit's filling the life. It is a distinct, personal, second crisis experience that every born-again believer can receive by faith in an instant. There is a cleansing of inward sin, and power to keep from sin, as well as perfect love to equip us for holy living.

Various names have been given to this experience: entire sanctification, perfect love, baptism with the Holy Spirit, Christian perfection, holiness of heart, and others. It is the gracious "gift of the Father" that Jesus prayed His followers would receive in John, chapter 17.

What are some of the hindrances and the privileges that earnest believers have in their quest for a life of victory and power to live above sin?

Our "Self" Is in the Way

It is amazing what can happen in real spiritual progress when we are set free from ourselves. Christ calls each of us out of our natural self-centeredness. He expects us to deal drastically with our old self-life. But so often we prefer to pander to our insidious self-interests. Oswald Chambers calls it giving up "our rights to ourselves," and for most of us it is a real struggle.

"Man is cursed with a BIG 'I' which will never be trimmed to size until completely recaptured, repossessed, and recontrolled by the Holy Spirit," suggests Richard Taylor. He explains that the "BIG I" is seen to be nothing other than the "law of sin," the "carnal mind," and the "evil heart of unbelief" with the mask off. Dr. Taylor says, "It is the disposition to relate everything to self and its interests, to a selfish and rebellious degree."[1]

The self-sufficient person says, "I want to serve God, but I'll do it my own way and in my own time." Paul speaks of the crucifixion of the sinful self in Gal. 2:20, then says: "And my present life is not that of the old 'I,' but the living Christ within me" (Phillips).

The ambitious longings of self and a heart full of pride will become to a Christian the ruling passion that strives to satisfy its feverish desires. Jean Stapleton, in her book *The Gift of Inner Healing,* says that pride is the barrier of self that thwarts, distorts, warps, and destroys the perfect love to which Christ calls and bids us come. She tells us that we cannot get out of the center of our universe unless we put Christ in the center. He must be there if we are to be whole.

Pride or Low Self-image?

I can hear someone saying, "Pride is not my problem— I have a low self-image, that's my big problem."

Ever since the Fall, people have suffered from either an inordinately high pride or an excessively low feeling of worthlessness.

"Pride is the root sin of man," said Augustine. By nature human beings have no sense of dependence on God, but rather an exaggerated sense of their own importance and pride in their own achievements. On the other hand, with an excessively low self-image, people look down on themselves, sometimes hate themselves, and think of themselves as worthless.

God does not intend for us to have either deviation. We do not have to bow at the altar of self. We can instead put self upon the altar. When God redeems us by His grace, He renovates our self-image in both directions. First, He gives us an honest awareness of our strengths and our weaknesses. We recognize that all our gifts and talents come from Him, and we are willing to use our gifts for Him and others. God helps us cultivate a true humility. Second, He corrects our low self-image by helping us grasp the tremendous resources He puts at our disposal. The Word of God gives us teachings on both justification and sanctification, and by faith we can build our faith toward a positive self-image. In Christ, we are no longer the same people. We have been changed.

As a young Christian I read a statement somewhere that said that I need not feel inferior to anyone, for I am attached to a superior God. I began to look at myself in the light of God's loving work of forgiveness and renewal.

The Christian's self-image means glorying in Christ, not in self. It is the opposite of spiritual pride. We are never satisfied with ourselves, but we are to press toward the goal of Christlikeness.

We must learn to see our life for what it truly is—not

ours by natural right to live any way we choose. But our life belongs to us only because God gave it to us, and we ought to live life in a way that He would choose.

Among my favorite quotes on the "self" are from C. S. Lewis's book *Beyond Personality.* He expresses so well the hindrance of our old "self-life":

> The more we get what we call "ourselves" out of the way and let Him take over, the more truly ourselves we become. . . . In that sense our real selves are all waiting for us in Him. It is no good trying to "be myself" without Him. It is when I turn to Christ, when I give myself up to His personality that I first begin to have a real personality of my own.[2]

Lewis goes on to explain the surrender of the "self."

> But there must be a real giving up of the self. You must throw it away blindly so to speak . . . the very first step is to try to forget about the self altogether. Lose your life and you will save it. Submit to death, death of your ambitions and favorite wishes every day. . . . Submit with every fibre of your being and you will find eternal life. Keep back nothing. Nothing in you that has not died will ever be raised from the dead. Look for yourself, and you will find in the long run only hatred, loneliness, despair, rage, ruin and decay. But look for Christ and you will find Him, and with Him everything else thrown in.[3]

Our self is not canceled when it is surrendered and consecrated to the Lord. It is heightened with a divine plus. We are not annihilated but cleansed by the Holy Spirit.

Our Master calls us to put whatever skills we possess into His great hands. When we do, our own self-importance does not interfere with the way He chooses to lead us. He then has the liberty to use us with enormous effectiveness.

The Fullness of the Spirit

As a young woman, not long after I had been converted, I realized the troublesome presence of my own sinful nature could not be tamed or suppressed. It needed to be cleansed and purified. When I heard Dr. Howard Hamlin speak on the sixth chapter of Isaiah, I knew that the raucous notes in my life had to be hushed forever. Willingly and decisively, I made a complete consecration to Christ. "Here, Lord, is my heart, my mind, my soul—all that I am and have—my family, my present, and my future. I am Yours, eternally and forever." I knew in that moment that the Comforter, the Holy Spirit, came to my heart with His indwelling presence. The Divine Master, with miraculous skill, had begun the wondrous work of attunement through heart cleansing. He took care of the sin that often made my personality a disorganized chaos. I, who once was so occupied with the claims of self, was now filled with the Spirit of the Living God. He flooded my heart with enormous joy and peace and most of all with love. My whole life was lifted to a higher plane, and I sensed a fresh enduement of power. Through the years there has been an intense desire for more of Him.

The experience of heart holiness is not a finality. It did not set me on a summit of ultimate spiritual privilege, nor did it make an angel out of me. But I have found it to be a stabilizing force, an establishing grace, a perfect preparation for my exploration of the riches of His grace. His presence by His Spirit is a living dynamic reality. And though living in a distraught and distracted world, the harmony of heaven and the melody of love belong to me!

> *Peace, perfect peace! Love, perfect love!*
> *Sweeping o'er my soul in heav'nly tides!*
> *Rest, perfect rest! Joy, perfect joy!*
> *is mine since the Holy Ghost abides.*
> —Rev. F. E. Hill

4

A Symphony of Truth

It was one of those fabulous summer evenings in June. We watched a gorgeous sunset on the horizon as we waited for the symphony to begin. Orange and purple hues of color stretched across the western sky. Tall pines along the esplanade were silhouetted against the sunset. The river sparkled with the reflection of the sun's rays.

Crowds of people began to seat themselves in lawn chairs around the open concert hall. Many spread blankets on the ground and stretched out comfortably. The orchestra was already seated. Players had been attentively tuning their instruments and were now ready to begin. When the famous conductor entered, the applause was thunderous. He bowed several times to the audience, then turned toward the orchestra and lifted his baton for the musicians to begin. Soon the melodious strains of the symphony began to fill the air. Music played—glad, joyous music—the richest rhythm, the sweetest melody. There was a principal theme running through the whole movement that was the source of the music. In the development of his theme and motives, the composer had achieved a masterly use of harmony, rhythm, dynamics, and instrumentation. Form had not been discarded. He made it subservient to his expressive desires.

I thought of the Divine Master. He proves His perfect mastery as He fits imperfect, human instruments to sound forth His praise. The instrument cannot tune itself. Our Maker tunes us by His mighty work of grace. He does much more than suppress our discordant elements. The personality that in the hands of Satan would have been a weapon, in the hands of God becomes a source of peaceful harmonies. However, His marvelous work of perfect tuning awaits our complete, irreversible self-committal into His hands. We then become "instruments of righteousness unto God." Thus our lives ring forth a symphony of truth.

As we fix our gaze upon Him for direction, our daily walk becomes rich and meaningful in a life of holiness. Our devotional times focus on knowing and loving Him. The spiritual disciplines, as a form, become a resource for growth and maturity in our development toward being like Him—Jesus, the Composer, our Conductor, our Theme—the Way, the Truth, and the Life. In the deepest sense, it is Christ in us—the living, contemporaneous Christ moving out into other lives. We find Him infinitely resourceful and able to make us more than a conqueror. He brings to our life a sense of energy, an overpowering vitality, an indescribable gusto, making us serenely and superbly adequate to meet life's demands.

Many Christians, however, live stagnated, powerless lives. They lack the joyous song—the rhythm of a daily walk with the Lord—a peaceful harmony. Becoming a Christian is one thing, and continuing in the Christian walk is another. A. W. Tozer wrote: "Probably the most widespread and persistent problem to be found among Christians is the problem of spiritual progress. Why after years of Christian profession, do so many persons find themselves no farther along than when they first believed?"[1]

The Spark That Ignites Intimacy

There are certain implications, responsibilities, and privileges that must concern us when we accept Christ as our Savior. He has not called us to a sloppy half-heartedness. It is serious business. We are called to a vigorous, absolute commitment. We are called to discipleship, and that means we are to learn and to obey Christ's instructions. Salvation is demonstrated by a life that goes on with God. Charles Colson wrote:

> Being Christian is more than mouthing pious hymns or believing in a vague deity. To follow the Christ of the Scriptures inevitably and radically—alters one's opinions and values on everything from life-style to the dignity of life, to justice, to art, to intellectual perceptions. It involves the totality of our lives—and only as we grasp that truth and make Christ Lord of all can we ever hope to make an impact of the totality of our culture.[2]

I needed to discover this concept for myself. I grew up in a liturgical church as a nominal Christian. I had a confused idea of what it meant to be a true Christian, and I embraced the world's values and attitudes. My church had all the paraphernalia of religion—the organization, the form, the machinery. But the vital spark, the creative, dynamic quality of life was missing. I did not really understand the meaning of the Cross, the way of salvation, the fact that redemption was provided for me personally. It was not until someone witnessed to me that I fully comprehended that I could be saved from my sins by my personal faith in Christ. When I surrendered my life to Christ, my spirit caught fire from His flame of love. He shattered my nominal Christianity and became a divine antidote to my dull, lusterless religion. Christianity became more than something I believed—it became something I acted upon. My deed, my practice, my discipline, the Divine Person himself—became my creed. He ignited my faith, and through the years I have kept it burning at His fire. Let me make it plain, however, that it has been my responsibility to walk in obedience to Him and to tend the fire that He kindled within—lest carelessness and indifference or neglect turn it into a pile of ashes.

A Growth Process

We believe in "growth in grace," not "growth into grace." Growth in grace is not spontaneous. It requires a faithfulness in details and perseverance when everything goes wrong. We develop sensitivity and devotion to Christ. We increasingly allow the Holy Spirit to control us. We intelligently detach from the things of this world, and we hold lightly our material possessions. Our spiritual life is dependent on the life-giving source of abiding in the vine. The goal then of our Christian life is to become more Christlike and to glorify God through knowing and loving Him. The hunger of the growing Christian's heart is echoed in the words of the songwriter:

Oh to be like Thee! blessed Redeemer,
This is my constant longing and prayer.

Frank Laubach, known as a modern mystic, speaks of his two burning passions: First, to be like Jesus. Second, to respond to God as a violin responds to the bow of the Master.[3]

Jesus is the perfect pattern for us. David Livingstone exclaimed, "He is the greatest Master I have ever known . . . the only Master supremely worth serving."

The Scriptures consistently admonish us to grow in the life of faith. As disciples of Jesus, we should be hungry for knowledge. The word *disciple* means "a learner"—one who learns from Jesus and responds with obedient action. Jesus said, "Take my yoke upon you and learn from me" (Matt. 11:29). James said, "Don't only hear the message, but put it into practice; otherwise you are merely deluding yourselves" (James 1:22, Phillips). If we fail to be "learners" in the Christian way, our growth process is stunted and our obedience hampered.

A Major Cause for Retarded Growth

How can we be active learners? How do we maintain the spiritual vitality of perpetual growth in order to stretch our minds and spirits? How can we avoid spiritual stagnation?

E. Stanley Jones said that spiritual growth is made or marred at the place of the devotional. He said, "It is the

crux. For in the devotional we expose ourselves to God's resources, we assimilate and grow by them."[4]

"The causes for retarded growth are many," explains
A. W. Tozer. "It would not be accurate to ascribe the trouble
to one single fault. One there is, however, which is so universal that it may easily be the main cause: failure to give
time for the cultivation of the knowledge of God."[5]

We can intensify our thirst for God if we promote a
learning process that will stimulate growth. First, we simply
must take time for quietness and reflection. There must be
time for God's Word and prayer. It takes time to be holy.
Our modern culture, with its emphasis on goal setting, pro-
grams us to face our tasks immediately. Our daily lives become a treadmill of activity; competing distractions fill our
homes. There are deadlines, meetings to attend, busyness,
haste. Many spend countless hours in pleasure and recre-
ation as compensation for life's stresses—rationalizing that
"they owe it to themselves." There is a great deal of activity
but so little accomplished toward the goal of knowing God
intimately and finding His power as the source of life. We
all need to relearn the Psalmist's suggestion, "Wait on the
Lord."

A. W. Tozer wrote: "Some things may be neglected but
with little loss to the spiritual life, but to neglect communion with God is to hurt ourselves where we cannot afford
it. God will respond to our efforts to know Him . . . it is al-
together a matter of how much determination we bring to
the holy task."[6]

Examine Our Priorities

There are no magic formulas that will help us know
and love God better. The real problem is priorities. Each of
us takes time for the things we feel are important. We must
come to the place in our lives where we let God know by
our words and actions: "Lord, You are the most important

person in my life. I cannot make it without You! So I dare not neglect You regardless of the urgencies of my life."

For years I wrestled over finding the best time for a satisfying devotional life. In college I tried often to awaken early but fell asleep on my knees. Of course, I didn't realize at the time the importance of getting to bed at a decent hour if I were going to keep my appointment with God in the morning without dozing.

I had been memorizing lines from E. Stanley Jones' *Abundant Living,* which I kept trying to apply to help me. He said, "It is best to have the Quiet Time in the pure, strong hours of the morning when the soul of the day is at its best." And, "Wash your thinking in the thought of Christ before you face the day."

Again, "Give your soul the fresh spring of the Morning Watch before you go to face the hard part of the day—the daily tasks and problems."[7]

After failing many times, I finally decided that I was not a "morning person" and that I would just have to find another time during the day. I soon learned that we cannot find time, nor will we have time to pray. We must decisively make time for prayer and God's Word.

It was not until I was a missionary that God helped me to have a fully satisfying devotional life. One morning I was awakened at 5 A.M. by the sound of music coming from the chapel. I heard the Bible school students singing in Creole:

"I must have the Savior with me for I dare not walk alone, / I must have His Presence near me and His arms around me thrown . . ."

An inner voice seemed to say to me, "You lazy missionary, lying there in bed while your students are awake seeking My face."

Throughout that day I thought a lot about the priorities of my life. Sure, I always prayed and read and studied the Bible. And I did know that the earlier I would have my devotions in the day, the more uniquely blessed my day would be. That day I prayed and asked God to help me, since I found that afternoons and evenings were so often easily eroded by unexpected people or activities and fatigue.

The next morning I awakened before my alarm sounded. I staggered to the kitchen, drank some orange juice and a cup of coffee, and made my way to the Bible school chapel before the sun was up. The morning air was stimulating, the heavens were "declaring the glory of God." In the chapel students were praying quietly in various places of the room. I knelt beside a bench and opened my Bible. It was a hallowed experience. There I touched the Divine Presence.

In those times I came to understand something of the majesty and splendor of the Almighty. Each morning I began to awaken automatically. Discipline became a delight. I sensed a new spiritual vigor. The growth process in my life was activated as never before. The habit was fixed. Every day that inner clock of the Spirit awakens me, and I jealously guard my time set apart for Him. For me, it has become the best time for Him to tune my heart to love Him, to learn of Him, to be motivated to obey Him. The prophet Isaiah says it beautifully: "The Sovereign Lord has given me an instructed tongue, to know the word that sustains the weary. He wakens me morning by morning, wakens my ear to listen like one being taught" (Isa. 50:4).

Do not misunderstand. God is not limited to meeting us only in the morning. Rising early has no special virtue. God will help you to know when your best time is to meet with Him. But when He shows you, make an effort to diligently keep your appointment. I have found morning to be the best for me. The important thing is that each of us decides by faith to make time for prayer and Bible reading and make it a priority of life over the other activities.

If morning is not your best time, at least commit your day and yourself to Him before you face the day with its battles, problems, or challenges. The Christian's daily life ought to be a continuous life of prayer. Someone said:

"True prayer is the constant appeal of our heart to God. It is our soul's unbroken song to the One who created us." We must not see the devotional life as separate from the rest of our day. But it is easier to keep that sustained devotion through the day when our communion has been first instructed and informed by the Scriptures and illuminated by the Holy Spirit. I like Dick Winn's definition of the devotional life. He said:

> At its very core "devotional life" is not a technique, a discipline, or a religious duty. It is the fascination of a person for a Person. It is the God-drawn questing of one's soul for the divine Friend by whom we were created for fellowship. As such, it has all the elements of an absorbing, rewarding mutual friendship.[8]

In establishing devotional goals, we should be open to God leading us in different ways and on different paths. As we develop habits in our devotional life we must beware of spiritual pride. Tozer reminds us that it is very easy to think that because we have prayed for an hour we have achieved something of merit. "If spiritual achievement is our goal," he said, "we have already replaced our openness to God's still voice with our own internal drive to succeed."

We are as individual in our spiritual needs as we are in our taste for our homes, our clothes, our books, or our hobbies. We cannot set down rigid rules except for the importance of finding an appropriate time and making it habitual.

John Wesley expressed it well when he said:

> I take religion to be, not the bare saying over of so many prayers, morning and evening, in public or in private; not anything superadded now and then to a careless or worldly life; but a constant ruling habit of soul, a renewal of our minds in the image of God, a recovery of the Divine likeness, a still increasing conformity of heart and life to the pattern of our most holy redeemer.[9]

The devotional life then is an attitude of constant desire to do God's will. Brother Lawrence described it this way: "God lays no great burden upon us . . . a little remembrance of Him from time to time, a little adoration; some-times to pray for His grace, sometimes to offer Him your sorrows, and sometimes to return Him thanks for the bene-fits He has given you. You need not cry very loud; He is nearer to us than we think."[10]

When a king asked Ole Bull, the celebrated violinist, where he caught the rapturous tones he brought out of his instrument, the artist replied, "I caught them, your Majesty, from the mountains of Norway." And so Christians who se-riously thirst to know God in a vital way must spend those times on the mount with Him if they expect to maintain harmony in the inner life. For no successful program of holy living can be provided impromptu on the public stage.[11]

> *Teach me to love Thee as Thine angels love,*
> *One holy passion filling all my frame:*
> *The baptism of the heav'n-descended Dove;*
> *My heart an altar, and Thy love the flame.*
> —GEORGE CROLY

5

Tuned to the Holy Spirit

The great scientist Charles Darwin recalled once that early in his life he had loved music and art and literature. He had a faculty for them and found intense delight in them; but because of his one-sided concentration on his scientific calculations, eventually he lost all taste for them. He wrote, "If I had my life to live over again, I would make it a rule to read some poetry and listen to some music at least once every week"—just to keep the faculty alive. If you and I neglect the Spirit of God with us, we, too, will lose our faculty of spiritual vision. A degeneration of our spiritual life will set in.[1]

Beauty of sound can be acquired and developed. The great composers placed much emphasis on the quality of tone. Debussy ordered that "every sound must be beautiful." Chopin insisted that one should practice on the best piano available and keep it in perfect tune to accustom the ear to the finest possible sound. If the Master musician has tuned our imperfect instrument, we will want to pursue a life of godliness by remaining in perfect tune to Him.

There is in our day a renewed interest in "spiritual formation" and a new emphasis on the devotional life. Many colleges and seminaries are offering a course in "spiritual formation." Articles on the spiritual disciplines have been appearing in Christian periodicals. New books on the devotional life are in demand. Could it be that our age increasingly realizes the need to be strengthened with inner resources in order to meet life's challenges?

There may be hidden dangers in some of the contemporary spiritual life movements. Therefore, we must heed the apostle John's advice, "Do not believe every spirit, but test the spirits to see whether they are from God, because many false prophets have gone out into the world" (1 John 4:1). Recently a lady described to me her meditation classes and the price she had to pay just to sit in a room by herself and think of nothing. We must learn to scrutinize private revelations and interpretations and search the Scriptures for the truth. God's Word simply must be the authority, the objective base, the standard of our spiritual life. When we as Christians begin to know Christ in a deep and radically renewing way, we will develop this experience into a lifestyle that will bear abundant spiritual fruit.

All great musician began as students who gradually assimilated their own concepts and experimented with musical thoughts. They learned from false starts and failure as well as from success. They developed their musical personality through knowledge and hard work. The most celebrated virtuoso and the most inexperienced student work with the same raw material, the printed score, the only true authority for the musician. For the Christian, the written authority is the Bible.

The spiritual disciplines can be filled with joy and song as we become more open and tuned continually to the Holy Spirit.

The Aim of the Spiritual Disciplines

The purpose of the disciplines in the life of the Spirit is to help us develop intimacy with our Lord. He wants us to enjoy His presence and to delight in His beauty. He can be our very present, unfailing Friend, closer than a brother, dearer than life, our very strength from day to day. Paul exclaimed one day in the public square of Athens, "For in him we live and move and have our being" (Acts 17:28). God knows the deep, innermost longings and desires of our hearts. He wants to give himself to the soul that really loves

Him. He will reveal himself to the one who earnestly seeks Him. The apostle Peter asks us: "Do you want more and more of God's kindness and peace? Then learn to know him better and better. For as you know him better, he will give you, through his great power, everything you need for living a truly good life: he even shares his own glory and his own goodness with us!" (2 Pet. 1:2-3, TLB).

A. W. Tozer, in his books, wrote much about knowing God. He said:

> Knowledge of such a Being cannot be gained by study alone. It comes by a wisdom the natural man knows nothing of, neither can know, because it is spiritually discerned. To know God is at once the easiest and the most difficult thing in the world. It is easy because the knowledge is not won by hard mental toil, but is something freely given. As sunlight falls free on the open field, so the knowledge of a holy God is a free gift to men who are open to receive it.[2]

If we are going to develop in our spiritual life, we must broaden our understanding of God and experience His divine truths. To know Him and to have a heart for Him is our greatest privilege. Our devotion toward Him means a reverent and loving desire for more of Him that finds its expression in wholehearted dedication to His service.

Richard Foster tells us that the purpose of the spiritual disciplines is "liberation from the stifling slavery to self-interest and fear." He says that when one's inner spirit is set free from all that holds it down, that can hardly be described as dull drudgery.[3]

John Wesley is an example of an intensely disciplined individual. For him every moment counted and was a "God-moment." His disciplines were meaningful and never an end in themselves. Daily he practiced the spiritual disciplines of prayer, Bible study, and devotion as the means to a vital relationship with God.

The spiritual disciplines should make us spontaneous, natural persons in the world—authentic, God-centered persons with a faith and theology that can be translated into creative, mature Christian living. The spiritual disciplines ultimately produce a life of satisfaction and enjoyment—a life of freedom. The law ends in a liberty. E. Stanley Jones exclaimed: "Freedom and discipline go together like the words and music of a song. There is no freedom without discipline."[4]

In times of prayer, solitude, and waiting on God in times of meditation and the reading of His Word, we develop a deeper spiritual perception. God has the opportunity to speak to us, to give us a vision of our task, and to reveal His will for us. We become more aware of and obedient to the inner voice that speaks in our conscience. We become more alert and sensitive to the mind of Christ. Our faith increases so that we take God at His word. We experience a supernatural love that sees in every human creature a brother or sister for whom Christ died. The result is a new dimension of the eternal. The spiritual disciplines are the instruments of joy—the way into mature Christian spirituality and abundant life. To neglect prayer and these special times with God will cause the faculty of spiritual vision to inevitably atrophy and decay. But an increased commitment to develop the Christian life, to know God better, will result in something warm and loving—not something hard and austere.

Time and time again, the Master comes alongside us in a gracious manner. He calls us from our busy world with a gentle invitation—never pushy, never rude, but eagerly expecting us to sense the call of His Spirit to our spirits. He awaits our response. And so we echo the sentiment in Amy Carmichael's little poem:

> Tune Thou my harp;
> There is not, Lord, could never be
> The skill in me.
>
> Tune Thou my harp,
> That it may play Thy melody,
> Thy harmony.

Tune Thou my harp,
O Spirit, breathe Thy
Thought through me
As pleaseth Thee.[5]

—AMY CARMICHAEL

From Loneliness to Creative Solitude

The funeral was over. The friends and relatives had left. My mother had died, and I was all alone in the house. World War II had just ended. My two brothers in Europe were hopeful of coming home from the army in a few months. Now a period of unwanted solitude was thrust upon me just as I turned 18. My job in the civil service office ended when the war did. My days seemed interminable.

I had been converted only a few months before. All my life I had been terribly afraid to be alone. While growing up, one of my brothers had filled me with horror stories of things that were going to happen to me. My imagination ran wild.

I realized it was now time to face my fears and to think about the direction of my life. I began to search the Scriptures and look to God. His gracious promise was true. He did not forsake me.

But Satan also decided to launch an all-out attack for my soul. A neighbor lady, steeped in spiritualism, came to convert me to her beliefs. The Jehovah's Witnesses, whom I had never heard of before, invited me to a Bible study, which I attended. An English teacher, whom I admired enormously, talked to me about her doctrine of Christian Science, though she did not call it by name. Confusion and questions began to fill my mind. A dark cloud hung low, and my newfound joy began to diminish.

One day a package arrived unexpectedly from England. It was filled with books—exciting Christian books—books I had never heard of nor seen. It was my first exposure to Christian literature. The package was from my brother anticipating his return home from the war. He had found the Lord and sent ahead the new books he had accumulated. To me they were like a gift from heaven. He had no idea what they would mean.

I began to read. Book after book began to give me a spiritual formation. They instilled a thirst for the knowledge of God and whetted my appetite to study His Word. My days became full. My fears dissipated.

The Christian Science teacher continued to confront me with her doctrine, but now I could question her and doubt her and argue with her. One day as I looked deeper into the treasure box of books, I pulled out a book titled *The Antidote to Christian Science.* The doctrine so carefully proclaimed and explained to me by the English teacher was there before me on the printed page, and the antidote given from the Bible.

A precious unseen presence filled the empty house and my lonely, grieving heart. I began to feel safe from all the darkness of cults. There was warmth, peace, comfort, stillness—and best of all God's love enveloping me. The light had extinguished the darkness. In the month-and-a-half that followed, I learned to search the Bible for answers to my dilemmas. My love for God increased. My mind became enlightened. I was becoming a true disciple of Jesus Christ, a "learner." He instilled within me a thirst for knowledge. The unwanted loneliness turned to creative solitude, to an eloquent silence, to contemplation, to the launching of my spiritual formation. My next step was to go to college.

William Barclay said:

> It is the law of the spiritual life that sooner or later a man must confront Jesus alone. It is all very well to take a decision for Jesus on the flood tide of emotion at some great gathering, or in some little group which is charged with spiritual power. But after the fellowship he must go back to the essential isolation of every hu-

man soul; and what really matters is not what a man does in the crowd but what he does when he is alone with Christ.[6]

"Islands of Solitude"

An outstanding piano teacher once remarked: "I was taught to 'listen,' first and foremost, as distinguished from 'hearing.' I was taught to learn from all sources with an open, credulous, and investigating mind and with the determination to make a piece 'sound right.'"

In the history of the Christian Church, times of solitude, silence, and listening have been referred to by the devotional masters as a spiritual discipline—a living experience to be pursued. It has often been referred to as inward prayer or contemplative prayer. Its purpose is to create the emotional and spiritual space that allows Christ to construct an inner sanctuary in the heart. Solitude and silence are inseparable. They have been the secret of the saints.

It was in times of solitude and listening, during His times of prayer, that Jesus learned the will of God. Before He began His ministry, this sociable individual spent 40 days all alone in the desert facing the forces of evil arrayed against Him. He spent the entire night by himself praying before He chose His 12 disciples. The Scriptures often speak of Jesus withdrawing from the crowds and going up in the hills by himself. He, too, had the limitations of common humanity and had to slip away from the thronging multitudes. Those intervals of silence and peace were important to Him.

Paul, after his conversion on the Damascus road where Christ was revealed to him, wrote in the Book of Galatians that he did not confer with any human being—but went away to Arabia. William Barclay said: "Paul went away to be alone. First, he had to think out this tremendous thing that had happened to him. Second, he had to speak with God before he spoke to men."[7]

Thomas à Kempis suggests that anyone who aims at inward and spiritual things must, with Jesus, turn aside from the crowd. Only the one who loves silence can safely speak.[8] Andrew Murray wrote: "Retire frequently with God into the inner chamber of the heart where the gentle voice of the Spirit is only heard if all be still."[9] Dietrich Bonhoeffer cautioned: "Beware of the person who does not have stillness and solitude in his life."[10] E. Stanley Jones spoke of the importance of "islands of solitude" without which we shall produce frantic personalities. He explains that as the body becomes tied up with physical tensions, so the soul becomes tied up in moral and spiritual tensions; and it is impossible to have a relaxed body if the mind and soul are full of conflict and tensions.[11]

As we listen to the Lord in times of silence, He helps us to gain new practical handles on life's ordinary problems. He helps us distinguish between the trivial and the significant. We feel better equipped to face our ordinary world with greater perspective and balance. We begin to develop an inner solitude of the heart that can be maintained at all times. The goal, then, of listening in the silence is to bring this stance of listening prayer into the course of our daily experiences—in the home, in the office, in the classroom— wherever we may be. We are attuned to the Holy Spirit's divine whisper. Thomas Kelly tells us that there is a way of ordering our mental life on more than one level at once. He said: "On one level we may be thinking, discussing, seeing, calculating, meeting all the demands of external affairs. But deep within, behind the scenes, at a profounder level, we may be in prayer and adoration, song and worship, and a gentle receptiveness to divine breathings."[12] Despite the noise and confusion about us, we are determined to settle into a deep inner peace and keep an inward attentiveness to Him.

A beautiful singer described the healing she found in

solitude after being at the point of exhaustion and failure in her career. Disheartened and discouraged, she wrote:

> I was still not sure I would ever sing again. For the first time in my life I had heard no music for three months. I had not whistled or hummed or sung a note. I think I was frightened to hear the sound that would come out of my abused voice. What was more terrifying was that I felt no music within me. I could not even re-call the joy of singing. But I was scheduled to make recordings with a group of gifted child singers.

She told how she went to the studio without working on the music. She was strangely calm. The children were gay and beautiful to look at. The moment came for them to blend their voices together. There was silence in the studio. The music began. The children's voices rose. And to her great joy she felt that glorious life-giving force from within, and she began to sing.

She said, "Like the fallow earth, my voice had rested, and I sang clearly and fervently. Like the fallow earth, the spirit within me soared. It is in solitude that we hear the voice of God."[13]

Let no one be mistaken about the discipline of solitude. As Thomas Merton reminds us: "The spiritual life is not a quiet withdrawal, a hot house growth of artificial ascetic practices beyond the reach of people living ordinary lives. It is in the ordinary duties and labors of life that the Christian can and should develop his spiritual union with God." Merton explains that when he gets away from people, however, and has an opportunity for an inner immersion into the silence of God, he emerges more sensitive to those around him. He feels that it is in deep solitude where he finds the gentleness with which he can truly love others.[14]

6

Forming a Biblical Score

God's Word can be an enormous power in our lives. The educator and Bible scholar Frank Gabelein, when asked by an editor of *Christianity Today* what counsel he would give the next generation, replied that we should maintain at all costs a daily time of Scripture reading and prayer. He said that looking back over 60 years, the most formative influence in his life and thought has been his daily contact with Scripture.

John Wesley referred to himself as "a man of one book." Martin Luther spoke of his conscience being a slave to the Word of God. Today our world is in great need of Christians who are thoroughly committed to biblical thinking and action.

We are often slow to read the portions of Scripture that require research and study. Many Christians, if they read at all, read only their favorite parts. There is an unwillingness to be stretched to study the more difficult texts. Charles Colson said: "It is obvious that we Christians are biblically illiterate, failing miserably to educate ourselves and defend our beliefs to others."[1] When we choose only selective readings of the Bible we shortchange ourselves by seeking for "immediate blessings." Let us not be impatient to hear God's voice in solitude or too distracted to diligently dig into His Word. The Bible is God's message to us. We need to know and understand that message.

Dr. Francis Schaeffer stated in his book *He Is There and He Is Not Silent:* "We should read the Bible for various reasons. It should be read devotionally. But reading the Bible every day of one's life does something else for you—it gives one a different mentality." He continues, "Do not minimize the fact that in reading the Bible we are living in a mentality which is the right one opposed to the great wall of this other mentality which is forced upon us on every side—in education, in literature, in the arts and in the mass media."[2]

The Bible is a standard of spiritual truth. In all the Holy Spirit's teachings and leading, He never contradicts His own Word. It is He who inspired the Scriptures, and He is the One who interprets and unfolds it to our heart. He makes the written Word power and reality and life to us. Just as musicians must work with the printed musical score, which is their only true authority, so must Christians depend upon God's Word to be the basis for all their beliefs—their doctrines, convictions, and standards. The Bible becomes more than a mere book; it must become our guide in life to which we look for direction in every move we make. It becomes both life and spirit, which energizes and propels us forward into every situation. As we form a biblical score for our lives, it will determine our conduct and our character.

Charles Colson writes: "Christianity rests on the belief that God is the source of truth and that He does not alter it according to the spirit of the times. When Christians sever their ties to absolute truth, relativism reigns, and the church becomes merely a religious adaptation of the culture."[3]

The Book of Proverbs exhorts us to "buy the truth and do not sell it; get wisdom, discipline and understanding" (23:23). When Jesus taught His disciples about the work of the Holy Spirit, He spoke of Him as "the Spirit of truth" and said that He would guide us into all truth (John 16:13).

John Wesley challenges us at the point of systematic reading of the Bible. He believes that Christians should know "the whole counsel of God." Steve Harper, in writing about Wesley's devotional life, points out the important questions that emerge for each of us. He asks:

> Am I reading the Bible in a way that brings me in contact with the whole of it? Do I read scripture in large

enough portions to see isolated passages in their larger context? Do I use responsible aids to add the insights of others to my study of God's Word? Do I have any means of marking, noting, and recording my discoveries?

Harper states: "In all these ways we are being true to Wesley's example which reminds us that an in-depth knowledge of scripture requires a systematic approach."[4]

The great preacher Charles Spurgeon said: "It is blessed to eat into the very soul of the Bible until, at last, you come to talk in scriptural language, and your spirit is flavoured with the words of the Lord, so that your blood is Bibline and the very essence of the Bible flows from you."[5]

The Strengthening Angel

Some years ago an emergency called me to Quito, Ecuador. My son, a missionary, had been in a horrible motorcycle accident and lay in a coma hovering between life and death. For more than a week his condition was precarious. There settled over me an awful sense of foreboding and fear. During my stay, while waiting for some improvement in his condition, his wife became desperately ill and had to be hospitalized. Sleep had not come easily for me while I was there, and I was completely exhausted. One night alone in the house I felt very strange and an eerie feeling prevailed over me. In the depths of my spirit I was devastated and felt there a desolating sense of human weakness. I could not pray. I could not think clearly. I could not read or sleep. Then at the crucial moment of strain, as I lay in bed, shining verses from God's Word began to pour into my heart and mind, reinforcing and rallying me. I suddenly felt new strength flow into me as though an angel had ministered to me. There was a fresh air of solace. The hidden treasures of His Word in my heart sustained me in that dark and critical moment.

James S. Stewart reminds us: "The Bible that we commonly ignore is really help from beyond. It is not a dull man-made compendium of religious theories and ideas. It is not one more tedious diagnosis of our dilemma and predicament. It is the real eternal world impinging on this world of sense and time. It is revelation. It is the strengthening angel."[6]

If the Bible is the foundation for your faith, you will find it to be a great source of inspiration in your life through the years. It will reveal to you the purpose of the Cross, God's will for your life, guidance when you begin to stray. It will be a stabilizing influence in your life. It will be a balm when you are wounded, and it will inspire a song in the night.

God's Word is the indispensable nourishment of our devotional life. We cannot live by bread alone. We must have words from the mouth of our Lord. Marvelous treasures of truth from the Bible can be realized only as we find and appropriate them by faith.

We need the same decisiveness that Martin Luther had about God's Word. We read from his poem:

I'll trust in God's unchanging Word
'Til soul and body sever;
For though all things shall pass away,
His Word shall stand forever.

The Art of Meditation

Times of meditation in the Christian's life can be a blessed experience. It can be a most helpful discipline in one's spiritual formation. It is a means of communing with God and getting to know Him better. The sacred writers sometimes called it "contemplative prayer." The songwriter knew what times of meditation meant when he wrote the song "In the Garden":

He speaks, and the sound of His voice
Is so sweet the birds hush their singing,
And the melody that He gave to me
Within my heart is ringing.

—AUSTIN MILES

Today, many have become suspicious of the word *meditation* because it makes us think of the Eastern religions and escapist cults of the New Age movement. Actually the Hebrews, who were an "Eastern" people, were well-versed in meditation and had a rich tradition of waiting on God and meditating.

References in the Scriptures on the subject of meditation usually refer to a spiritual process of dwelling on the Lord—His Word, the precepts, the law of the Lord, His creation, His beauty. It is a means of entering into the living presence of God to worship, praise, and adore Him.

There are those who would make meditation something very difficult or complicated. One does not have to be a religious professional or a spiritual giant to practice meditation. It is really very simple and should become as natural as breathing—a basic human activity for the Christian.

First of all, let's understand that Christian meditation is not psychological manipulation. It is not a method of controlling the brain waves in order to improve our physiological and emotional well-being. It is not losing our personhood and individuality as some of the Eastern religions would stress. It is not an unhealthy other-worldliness that makes us immune to human suffering.

Meditation is a way of thinking. It is disciplined concentration or focusing on the Lord—on His Word, His splendor, and His majesty. The Quakers call this focusing, "a centering down." It is a way of delighting in the Lord, a way of experiencing God and listening to Him. Paul encourages us in Phil. 4:8 to think or to meditate on the good things, the true things, the lovely things, the pure and honest things—the positive things. How many times our minds turn toward negative ideas that bring us down and keep us out of the stream of the Spirit.

Thomas Merton wrote:

> To meditate is to think. And yet successful meditation is much more than reasoning or thinking. It is

much more than "affections," much more than a series of prepared "acts" which one goes through. In meditative prayer, one thinks and speaks not only with his mind and lips, but in a certain sense with his whole being . . . it is the orientation of our whole body, mind and spirit to God in silence, attention, and adoration. All good meditative prayer is a conversion of our entire self to God.[7]

When we decide to spend time in meditation, distractions will be inevitable. "A heart that is used to the exterior life of noise and worry and haste will find it difficult at first to turn all that off and enter into the soul of God," said Tozer.[8]

When we do have time for meditation, we often decide to fill up space with anything we can: some other task, a phone call, a book, a shopping trip—anything that makes us feel we're doing something or accomplishing something. But the key to managing the distractions is in our attitude toward them. They are entirely manageable if we begin to occupy ourselves with total devotion to God. Every disruption can be converted into an amazing opportunity to visit what Meister Eckhart and Thomas Kelly called "the inner sanctuary"—a place deep within us to which we may continuously return.

Christian meditation can be done in a variety of ways, but most techniques include a period of reflection on Scripture. Meditation engages our affections and awakens within us a desire to enjoy God's presence and fellowship.

In Exodus 33, we read how Moses pitched a tent outside the camp when the people were wandering through the wilderness. It was called "the tent of meeting." When Moses went inside this tent, God's pillar of cloud would come down and stay at the entrance while the Lord spoke with him. Verse 11 says: "The Lord would speak to Moses face to face, as a man speaks with his friend." In this chapter we see one of God's revelations of His nature and what God means by His glory. Times of meditation can help us to catch a glimpse of the holiness of God.

Meditation will produce a longing for God himself. Note how the Psalmist expresses this desire over and over again. In Ps. 42:1-2 he says: "As the deer pants for streams of water, so my soul pants for you, O God. My soul thirsts for God, for the living God. When can I go and meet with God?" How intense is the hunted deer that thirsts for water.

Again in Ps. 63:1, the Psalmist illustrates the intensity of his desire for God's presence: "O God, you are my God, earnestly I seek you; my soul thirsts for you, my body longs for you."

In Ps. 27:4, David speaks of the *one* thing he wants from God. It is: "to gaze upon the beauty of the Lord." I like the way *The Living Bible* makes this passage sparkle. It says: "the privilege of meditating in his Temple, living in his presence every day of my life, delighting in his incomparable perfections and glory."

In the New Testament, Paul expressed the same intensity of desire in Phil. 3:10. He said: "I want to know Christ." The *Amplified Bible* says: "[For my determined purpose is] that I may know Him—that I may progressively become more deeply and intimately acquainted with Him, perceiving and recognizing and understanding [the wonders of His person] more strongly and more clearly."

The devotional masters often wrote of developing the habit of "inwardly gazing upon God" or "beholding Him"— meaning a sweet communion always going on. George MacDonald feels that we remain creeping Christians because instead of looking at Christ, we look at ourselves. Meditation is the practice of looking at Jesus and being captivated by Him.

We must be aware that another person's method is unlikely to be exactly right for us. We cannot have someone else's experiences or someone else's spirituality. Too many of the modern meditation techniques are an end in themselves. As long as knowledge of God is the goal, meditation can be a very useful devotional practice. Richard Foster stated:

"The Spiritual Disciplines are an inward and spiritual reality and the inner attitude of the heart is more crucial than the mechanics for coming into the reality of the spiritual life."[9]

In periods of meditation we worship God. We adore Him. We love Him. We bask in the warmth and light of His presence. God in turn comes to us in His own gracious and generous ways and lovingly unfolds newer and richer perceptions of His truths. He develops our capacity to understand and trust Him and imparts an imperturbable peace to our lives.

Meditation should result in richer and more loving relationships and make a difference in the quality of our lives.

"The end of the Christian discipline is to hide it away into habit," said E. Stanley Jones, "into the subconscious, so that the disciplined person appears to be and is spontaneous. A musician's creative spontaneity is coordinated discipline which has become second nature."[10]

Frank Laubach, in his book *Letters by a Modern Mystic,* wrote of his inner experiences of meditating and cultivating God's presence. He tells of the changes that were made in him as well as the changes of the attitudes of people toward him. Laubach said: "I feel, I feel like one who has had his violin out of tune with the orchestra and at last is in harmony with the music of the universe."[11]

Keeping a Personal Journal

Journaling can become the launching point for a continuous program of inner disciplines. It has been a rich experience for many. The journal is a personal growth tool. As they record significant thoughts and emotions, many people have discovered within themselves resources they did not know they possessed. The keeping of a journal is a way of charting one's spiritual progress.

Journal keeping helps us to identify our own personal needs. We can reevaluate our behavior by reflecting, praying, and finding direction. We come to know ourselves better. It is a way of listening to God and recording the truths He shares with us. It's a way of taking time out for ourselves and allows a sort of meditation to take place or a personal conversation with the Lord. It gives opportunity to verbalize our feelings: to express our problems and struggles or to record our joys and inspirations. The journal can include ideas and records of events that make up our life.

Many people feel self-conscious about writing in a journal. They are afraid to look into their own emotions and experiences. They may even be afraid to reveal their real selves. It is true that journal writing does demand a personal honesty and openness before God.

Journaling follows no rules. Author Ruth Vaughn, in her book *Write to Discover Yourself,* speaks about the diary/journal in which one may record the daily events and activities in addition to the journal as a personal growth tool. Ruth says:

> My challenge to you is to approach the diary/journal as your best friend in the world. You can pour out things here you might not dare to say to anyone else. . . . This is not for publication in the *Reader's Digest.* This is *you* taking Thoreau's advice to "Direct your eye right inward" and travel the "thousand undiscovered regions in your mind." And for such a journey, you cannot have the slightest concern for correct form, neatness, or intelligibility to anyone except yourself and God. And, in later reading, some of it may be decipherable only to God . . . but that is all right! Even the illegible gives you a "feel" for the tumult of your heart at that moment. And that is a recording within itself.[12]

Keep a notebook and pen ready to write during a "quiet time" with the Lord. This gives you a sense of expectancy and anticipation of receiving some word from Him. When reading Scripture or a devotional book, record your opinions, ideas, and thoughts as you reflect on what you have read. If you do not write your inspiration down, it will fade out quickly.

I especially like to record quotes or prayers from the devotional masters or great Christians. In fact, I have found my journal a useful reference to me in the writing of this book.

When you write, write how you feel and not how you think you should feel. Your journal will be more valuable to you if you get at the feeling level when you write. Include your feelings about what happened. Let your emotions get into your journal; don't protect the page. If you write from this level, you will diffuse the feelings and you will see them objectively.

Make your journal what you want it to be. Others may give suggestions or advice, but follow your own instincts in what you want. Experiment with your journal—the kind of notebook you use, the time at which you write, or the place where you write.

Some people find a prayer diary very helpful. Some like to write out their prayers, which helps them concentrate and keep their minds from wandering. In my journal I keep a prayer list and prayer requests. Then I indicate the date when prayers are answered.

Try dialoguing with a spiritual classic. Read, record, and reflect upon the gems of spiritual truths that have been tried and tested by the devotional masters. Try Augustine, Brother Lawrence, Thomas à Kempis, Evelyn Underhill, François Fénelon, Thomas Merton, Thomas Kelly, Madame Guyon, and others.

Some of my friends like to paraphrase the scripture they are reading that day. One spiritual exercise that I enjoyed was to journal the entire Book of James. I read it in four translations in one volume and recorded the verses from the translation that appealed to me that day. I would journal until God told me to do something in obedience to Him. Then I recorded my reflective comments about the scripture following my entry that day and set out to obey Him. Rereading some of those pages in my journal has been interesting to see the lessons God taught me from His Word.

Use your journal to record your goals—short-range

and long-range. This can be a help in clarifying your major life purposes.

Susan Annette Muto makes some significant comments about journal keeping:

> Journaling is one of the most helpful exercises we can do to increase our capacity for meditation and prayer. Pausing daily or a few times a week to jot down our thoughts has a way of quieting and uncluttering our overactive, decentered lives. Writing helps us to work through detected obstacles to spiritual living. . . . A journal is not only a record of events that touch and transform us; it is a private space in which we can meet ourselves in relation to others and God.[13]

7

Joy—the Crescendo of Inner Harmony

There was no question about it. It was Beethoven's Fifth Symphony that was playing as I turned on the classical radio station. The music played on and began to rise to a magnificent crescendo and ended in a blaze of glory. I wondered, What makes a composition a work of art? What is the special quality that starts a chain of inspiration and stays with the listener? It is amazing how music stimulates creative thought on its own. There have been thousands of performances of Beethoven's symphony—still it remains fresh. For one-and-a-half centuries it has remained popular. The joyous music lifts our spirit. The creative fire continues to kindle the imagination and stir emotion in all of us. With music like that it is impossible to miss the spirit of genuine art.

I thought about God. Humanity itself is a work of art fashioned by our great Creator. We are God's crowning creation. According to the Book of Job, God's work of creation was done to musical accompaniment. What kind of music? It seems that stars blended together in music that resembled song.

God asks: "Where were you when I laid the earth's foundation? Tell me, if you understand. Who marked off its dimensions? Surely you know! . . . On what were its footings set, or who laid its cornerstone—while the morning stars sang together and all the angels shouted for joy?" (Job 38:4-7).

God made us for himself that we might have fellowship with Him and experience complete fulfillment. His original purpose for us—His divine intention—was joy. He was interested in our happiness. When sin entered the world, sorrow entered with the loss of the sense of God. As we find God, so joy is restored—restored to communion with God and to the place of joy. Christ's atonement removed the barriers to the divine fellowship. Now in Christ we are objects of God's delight. He enfolds us to himself with an inexpressible joy.

"The Lord thy God in the midst of thee is mighty; he will save, he will rejoice over thee with joy; he will rest in his love, he will joy over thee with singing" (Zeph. 3:17, KJV).

Joy is an essential part of God's character. He is known as "the God of all joy." It has been said that joy is a lubricant for our belief and faith. Norman Vincent Peale speaks of joy freeing the mind and unlocking the muscles. He believes that a truly joyful person is in God's rhythm A doctor once told him that the internal system of blood and heart and organs in the human body functions in rhythm. And rhythm can be another word for harmony. Harmony can be another word for joy. Therefore when we are joyful, we are in rhythm.[1] God knows exactly what we need for inner harmony.

Jesus told His disciples during the Olivet Discourse that His joy would remain in them and that His joy would be complete. Joy has always been a significant hallmark of the Christian's life. E. Stanley Jones said: "Joy is the strength of the people of God; it is their characteristic mark. If there is no real joy, there is no real Christianity. For Christianity is life set to music."[2]

We must never allow the enemy to suggest to us that being a Christian is the limitation of joy. The world with all its allurements cannot compare to the real joy that comes to the heart delivered from sin and guilt.

The concept "joy" appears in the Scriptures in a variety of forms such as "joyful," "rejoice," "joy of the Lord," or "joy in the Holy Spirit." The Christian's joy is not the kind of emotion caused by great delight or happiness because of outward circumstances. We all know what it feels like to be happy because everything is going well—a bubbling, effervescent exuberance. That kind of joy does not last. Teaching that a "happy" feeling is a necessary characteristic of a good Christian can cause great discouragement or guilt. E. Stanley Jones defines joy this way: "The Christian joy is a joy from a sense of well-being, of harmony with the sum total of reality, of feeling the music of the spheres singing its way through our own souls, of direct and immediate contact with His joy."[3]

Joy in the Midst of Trials

I have known many Christians who have gone through great trials or suffering, but they still maintained a joy—a divine dimension in their life that was not based on circumstances or people. Christians have a hidden spring in their life that comes from the presence of God. Here is where they find the source of their joy. It is a result of relationship. There is a deep, settled sense of contentment that comes from knowing that God is in control. Teilhard de Chardin said, "Joy is the most infallible sign of the presence of God."

The quickening influence of the Holy Spirit permeates the entire life. Joy is a fruit of the Spirit. The apostle Paul could write: "We are hard pressed on every side, but not crushed; perplexed, but not in despair; persecuted, but not abandoned; struck down, but not destroyed" (2 Cor. 4:8-9).

Paul also coined the paradox, "Sorrowful, yet always rejoicing."

Reading a devotional book written by Watchman Nee, I came across this letter he wrote, dated April 22, 1972, in his 69th year. He had been confined for 20 years and shortly before his death he wrote:

> You know my physical condition. It is a chronic illness—it is always with me. When it strikes, it causes pain. Even if it should be dormant, it is nonetheless there. The difference is whether it strikes or not. Recov-

ery is out of the question. In summer the sun can add some color to my skin, but it cannot cure my illness. But I maintain the joy in me. Please don't be anxious. I hope you will also take good care of yourself, and be filled with joy! All the best to you.[4]

Joy in Unfavorable Circumstances

People who consistently live by the joy and praise and faith pattern of thinking seem to achieve a remarkable mastery over circumstances.

I was sitting on a bench beneath a thatched-roof church in a Sunday evening service in the interior of Haiti. It was a dark night, and the Coleman lamp flickered throughout the service. In the middle of the service I suddenly felt dizzy and could feel myself sliding off the bench. I thought I was going to pass out. I became aware that the thatched-roof above me was swaying back and forth and that the whole audience was trying to hold on to their seats to keep from falling. We were having an earthquake. My first impulse was to run out of the building into the darkness of the night. All of a sudden a young woman managed to get to her feet and literally staggered to the front of the church. She began to sing:

> Anywhere with Jesus I can safely go,
> Anywhere He leads me in this world below.
> Anywhere without Him dearest joys would fade.
> Anywhere with Jesus I am not afraid.

In that moment I felt it was the sweetest music ever to come to my ears, for the most beautiful spirit and calm settled down on the fear-gripped audience. This young woman had learned the secret of a singing heart. And the lesson I learned in those moments of panic was this: If a young Christian could learn to sing the song of joy under such circumstances, I am safe in affirming that anyone in any circumstance can learn it. It is faith that makes joy possible, not our circumstances.

Joy in Service to God and Man

On the walls of Moody Hall in Chicago were these words: "The greatest joy in life is to make Jesus Christ known." Anyone who has led a soul to Jesus Christ will agree there is no joy that compares to this. It is no wonder the Scriptures tell us that even "the angels in heaven rejoice over one sinner that repents."

The person who gives his or her life to help others is blessed by a deep joy in the Lord. We are all captivated by the stories and illustrations of Mother Teresa who received a Nobel prize for her selfless devotion to India's teeming multitudes of the poor. In her book *A Gift for God,* she demonstrates that joy is simply carrying out God's will in the common way of daily experience. She writes:

> Joy is prayer—Joy is strength—Joy is love—
> Joy is a net of love by which you can catch souls.
> She gives most who gives with joy.
> The best way to show our gratitude to God and to the people is to accept everything with joy. A joyful heart is the inevitable result of a heart burning with love.[5]

Leo Tolstoy was right when he said: "Joy can be real only if people look upon their life as a service, and have a definite object in life outside themselves and their personal happiness."[6]

When Christians love, give, help, and serve—their love will deepen, and their love for God and His world will measurably increase.

A few months ago I received a letter from a friend, a pastor's wife who moved to a large metropolitan city in the west. In her letter to me she wrote of the joy she experienced in the new but difficult assignment. Despite the surrounding environment, she and her husband sought to reach out to their world. I quote from her letter:

> The Lord is really blessing us. We've had some new families come and a couple of singles. Living in this city

is very different. Recently I met a street dweller, took her home, fed and bathed her, and gave her warm clothes to wear. I met another lady one day who lived a block and a half away. I felt led to witness to her. She promised to come to church. Then later she told me she is a man. I thought something was strange. The police came to the church and day-care and had mug shots for us to look at. This person is wanted by the police. This certainly is a different world! But the desert is in bloom!

Author C. S. Lewis had much to say about "joy" in his writings. He used phrases such as "surprised by joy"—like a flash of lightning on a dark and stormy day; or "stabs of joy"—meaning momentary glimpses that both satisfy and at the same time set one longing. Lewis wrote of God calling His children not only to right practices but also to the only genuine happiness, joy. He remarked: "If the face of the coin is obedience, its other side is the continuous recognition that God is, and that He is my Creator and Savior. Whatever my daily circumstance, His joy is to remain in me forever."[7]

The Joy of Obedience

When I walked into the classroom, I could tell instantly from the glum look on Elaine's face that she had fallen back into her old sinful habits. She sat in my Sunday School class with her eyes averted, her facial expression drawn, and her head drooping. There was a marked difference from her usual responsiveness to the lesson. It was apparent to me that she had lost the joy of her salvation.

Later as we talked she exclaimed, "I just can't live this Christian life! You can't understand my environment. There are just too many temptations for me."

I talked to her about the importance of quick recovery—that John speaks of in his letter: "If anybody does sin, we have one who speaks to the Father in our defense—Jesus Christ, the Righteous One. He is the atoning sacrifice for our sins" (1 John 2:1). Then I went on to explain that the life of obedience is a momentary life. It is a succession of little acts and habits and victory that fill the moments. God can give us grace each moment to trust Christ and by steadily, faithfully obeying Him the habit of obedience is formed. There is no simple, easy way to instant godliness, but as we daily obey what God tells us to do, the obedient life becomes a part of us.

All of us need continually to remind ourselves that everything in the Christian life hinges on obedience—absolute, implicit, and unquestioned obedience. Phillip Keller states: "Emotional experience is no substitute for the knowledge of the true and living Lord Jesus Christ. He can be known only by obedience to His Word. That is the ultimate test of truth."[8]

The subject of obedience has such a large part in the teachings of Jesus. It was a requirement for His followers: In His last days with them, He reminded them:

"If you love me, you will obey what I command" (John 14:15).

"Whoever has my commands and obeys them, he is the one who loves me. He who loves me will be loved by my Father, and I too will love him and show myself to him" (John 14:21).

"If anyone loves me, he will obey my teaching" (John 14:23).

"He who does not love me will not obey my teaching" (John 14:24).

"If you stay in me and obey my commands, you may ask any request you like, and it will be granted!" (John 15:7, TLB).

"If you obey my commands, you will remain in my love" (John 15:10).

"You are my friends if you obey me" (John 15:14, TLB).

We cannot call ourselves disciples of Jesus apart from obedience. The formula for our Christian life is "hearing

Christ's words," then "doing them." This brings spiritual success and deep, personal joy. It takes a deliberate setting of the will, a determination of the spirit to live each day with an openness to God's still voice.

C. S. Lewis writes: "There are only two kinds of people in the end: those who say to God, 'Thy will be done,' and those to whom God says, in the end, 'thy will be done.' All that are in Hell, choose it. Without that self-choice there could be no Hell."[9]

Full commitment to our Lord gives Him the "right of way." His life is released through us in all the freshness and power of divine action. His joy sweeps through all the channels of our being. "And when we obey him, every path he guides us on is fragrant with his lovingkindness and his truth" (Ps. 25:10, TLB).

8

Sounds of Praise and Worship

Amy sighed, irritation showing in her eyes. "I'm just tired of going to that church and not getting a blessing," she blurted out. "I just haven't been getting anything out of the services, and I feel that I need to look for another church that will meet my needs."

"But, Amy," I replied, "worship isn't really for us to get a blessing. It is for us to give God an acceptable sacrifice of praise. It is our response to God's love. He wants us to worship Him 'in spirit and in truth.' We may sing and praise and pray to God, but worship occurs only when His Spirit touches our spirit. We need to put something into a worship service if we expect to get something out of it."

True worship is adoration and admiration of a Holy God—"high and lifted up." Christ is the leader of our worship, who reveals himself to us. He speaks to us in the depths of our being—teaching, comforting, rebuking, or guiding. Worship is a time to behold Him and to open ourselves to His presence.

There are many people who see religion selfishly. They treat the gospel as a kind of prescription to secure them against what may be difficult or disagreeable. Some think a worship service should always give them an emotional high; or that it is something to help them relax. To view religion as something self-centered and introverted is to miss the true meaning of worship. It is true that as we seek for new insights into God's Word and seek for more of God himself, as we seek for creative ways to serve Him and others—then the emotional reactions will follow.

If we have difficulty with worship, perhaps it is because we have a wrong view of God and have never developed a sense of His awesomeness, holiness, and majesty. Have we become too flippant or complacent? Are we too familiar with God, lacking the reverence that His Being demands? A right concept of God is basic to our worship and to practical Christian living as well. Reverence is the source of godliness in us.

God will reveal himself to us as we worship Him rightly. He longs to communicate His presence to us. We must come before Him in humility, sensing our unworthiness and letting our self-sufficiency dissipate. On a flyleaf of my Bible I have penned a quote I memorized from one of Phillip Keller's books: "In the presence of the Prince of Peace dying on the Cross for me, my petty pride is pulverized. My self-esteem evaporates. The best I have appears as absolutely nothing."

Worship will produce an effect upon the worshipers. Though the object of our worship is God and its sole aim His glory, there will be a spiritual union of affection and likemindedness. God's will and God's holiness will become our greatest desire. Worship and life are linked together. True worship needs a response so that we may go out to face life with all its uncertainties. Because we worship, we go with greater confidence and obedience to answer His call to service.

Personal and private worship is important, but we also need the discipline of corporate worship. We need the encouragement and challenge of fellow believers. And there is a wonderful sense of joy in the fellowship of God. The writer to the Hebrews wrote: "Let us consider how we may spur one another on toward love and good deeds. Let us not give up meeting together, as some are in the habit of doing, but let us encourage one another" (10:24-25). Christ has promised to be in our midst—our risen Lord is alive and wants to bless us. Through worship we discover that there is one thing we need—to know Him.

How Is Your Praise Life?

Recently we studied the Book of Ephesians in my Sunday School class. We noted that Paul did not always separate praise from theology. Though Ephesians is rich in doctrinal truths, it also reads like a hymn: "Praise be to the God and Father of our Lord Jesus Christ, who has blessed us in the heavenly realms with every spiritual blessing in Christ" (1:3). Paul helps us experience something of that eternal praise to which Christ calls us, that "we . . . might be for the praise of his glory" (v. 12). His response was one of gratitude, thanksgiving, and praise as he reflected on who God is and what He had done for him.

All of us need to find the moments throughout each day to lift our hearts in praise to our Heavenly Father. There are a thousand things for which to express our gratitude. He has designed our world with all its exquisite beauty and loveliness—the whole earth speaks His glory. As we exalt Him, He will speak to us with clarity and attune our spirit with His. It is amazing what refreshment and renewal we will receive in our moments of praise and joy.

Do you ever sing your praises to the Lord? A hymnbook is indispensable to me in my devotional times with the Lord. When my own words fall short in expressing my deep feelings to the Lord, I sing a hymn such as:

> *O for a heart to praise my God*
> *A heart from sin set free,*
> *A heart that always feels Thy blood*
> *So freely shed for me!*
> —Charles Wesley

Making Melody to the Lord

Paul also tells us: "Let the word of Christ dwell in you richly as you teach and admonish one another with all wisdom, and as you sing psalms, hymns and spiritual songs with gratitude in your hearts to God" (Col. 3:16). When His Word dwells in us, our character and life-style increasingly reflect Him, and teaching, admonishing, and singing flow from us naturally.

Paul mentions several types of Christian praise songs. The first is a "psalm," which is an Old Testament scripture song. These were usually accompanied with a musical instrument and reflect on the character of God and His Word. The second kind of song is a "hymn." This refers to a song with a Christian theme that is addressed to God. In a hymn we tell God how much we love Him and appreciate His character and mighty works through Christ. The third category mentioned is a "spiritual song." This may be an old favorite or a contemporary chorus. The key is not musical style but spiritual content.[1]

Simplicity and modern choruses seem to be the order of the day in many churches. Yet, we must never ignore completely the traditional forms of the old hymns that express the continuity of our faith. There is a timelessness of God's covenants with His people. Many people today argue that we cannot keep singing the old hymns, for they are not relevant to the new people coming to our churches. We need to remember that we are making disciples instead of inspiration junkies. Disciples are people accustomed to discipline. Don Hustad refers to some of the choruses as being "as short and encapsulated as news stories and as repetitive as fast food commercials." Yet, choruses, too, have a place and can bring a joy or a lilt to our services. But a steady diet of choruses can leave us lacking in the expression of the great theological truths of our faith.

Whatever style, our attitude as we sing should be one of grateful worship. Praise is both our recognition of God's gracious character and our expression of worship to Him from our innermost feelings.

Finding Creative Ways to Praise God

Out of the stirrings of joy that come from obedience and communion with God, praise wells up in our emotions. But until we learn to verbalize it, we cannot experience it in its fullness. Praise extends us to a world beyond ourselves as we reach upward in thought of our loving Heavenly Father—our Great Creator.

How we human beings crave love and affection! How we shine when someone appreciates us or bestows a compliment at just the right time. Praise motivates us to be better than we are. What child hasn't felt like a million dollars when discovered doing something right and being praised for it? But praise to God is more than compliment, approval, or the giving of honor. C. S. Lewis suggests that it is in the process of being worshiped and praised that God communicates His presence to men. He writes:

> But for many people at many times the "fair beauty of the Lord" is revealed briefly or only while they worship Him together. Even in Judaism the essence of the sacrifice was not really that men gave bulls and goats to God, but that by their so doing God gave himself to men; in the central act of our own worship, of course, this is far clearer—there it is manifestly, even physically, God who gives and we who receive.[2]

Praise originates with God. The joy He gives springs up and floods us with contentment. However, we are such self-conscious people that often we cannot praise God publicly. Not until we become more God-conscious and aware of His intervention in all our affairs will we be able to praise Him adequately. The expression of our praise must be learned.

"Let the redeemed of the Lord say so, whom He has redeemed from the hand of the enemy" (Ps. 107:2, NKJV).

Praise cannot arise from a wrong spirit or a negative

attitude. There must be love for all people and all creation. Joy will then permeate our spirits seeking expression.

Madame Guyon wrote: "Your life is fascinating, with pleasant surprises everyday. Praise [God] for the richness of the life [He has] given you. Each time you feel a negative attitude building up inside yourself, refuse to accept it. Recognize the source of it, reject it, and turn to [Him]."[3]

Suggestions for Introducing Praise into Your Life:

1. Begin by reading the Psalms and collecting verses that describe how you feel toward God.

2. Write down the qualities that amaze you about God. For example, when I think of God as Sustainer of the universe, I am overwhelmed with praise. The fact that He cares for all His creation and provides for them, whether they ever bow the knee to Him or not, is utterly amazing.

3. Remember on a regular basis all the wonderful things God has done for you. The Scriptures warn us about the actions of the children of Israel: "They quickly forgot His works; . . . They forgot God their Savior, Who had done great things in Egypt, Wonders . . . And awesome things." Because of forgetting what God had done, "they despised the pleasant land; . . . grumbled in their tents; . . . did not listen to the voice of the Lord. . . . they provoked Him to wrath, . . . were rebellious against His Spirit," and they then went into sin (Ps. 106:13, 21-22, 24-25, 32-33, NASB).

4. Cultivate the attitude of thankfulness. One of the best ways to do this is to recognize that "Every good and perfect gift is from above" (James 1:17). Learn to be content with what you have. See each day, each breath as a gift from God. Every moment can have sacred relevance.

5. Put a rein on your mind and tongue. "Take captive every thought to make it obedient to Christ" (2 Cor. 10:5).

6. Learn to praise God frequently throughout the day. The Psalmist said, "Seven times a day I praise you for your righ-

teous laws" (119:164). When we awaken in the night, let His praise be on our minds and tongue. Someone said, "A genuine living faith sings divine songs in the night." Throughout the day, pause to let Him know how much you love Him. How we love Fanny Crosby's poetic expression: "This is my story, this is my song, / Praising my Saviour all the day long."

As we learn to praise God, in spite of what may happen to us, we are not giving the enemy a foothold in our life. Praise defeats the enemy's power over our life and helps master the spirit of discouragement and despair. "What shall I render to the Lord for all His benefits toward me?" the Psalmist asks (116:12, NASB). Then he responds: "I will offer to you the sacrifice of thanksgiving, and will call upon the name of the Lord" (v. 17, NKJV).

Samuel Medley, the songwriter, wrote:

> *O could I speak the matchless worth,*
> *O could I sound the glories forth*
> *Which in my Saviour shine.*

PART THREE

Minor Chords

9

Eliminating the Discords

"This is the day of the big sound," exclaims Dr. Richard Taylor. "Sometimes it is hypnotic and overpowering."[1] It is true that if we listen for very long, we are bound to hear jarring discords and harsh janglings that can be nerve-racking to one who is not accustomed to the disturbing elements. We are bombarded by music forms that encourage sensuality and recklessness. The relentless beat of some music, if allowed, can distract God's people from the things of His Spirit. But there are many other music forms available to us that stimulate awareness of beauty, or moods of pensiveness and aspiration. Music can make us joyous and lift our spirits. It can make our heart leap eagerly until we are awestruck by the glory surrounding us. Music is a living language, more eloquent than any spoken tongue.

I like to think of the Christian life as a life lived in a harmonious relationship with God and man. There is a striking verse in Rev. 15:2 where the apostle John, in his vision, sees the redeemed of the Lord victorious over the beast. They are standing beside the glassy sea, and they have harps given them by God. They sing the song of Moses the servant of God and the song of the Lamb.

Dr. H. Orton Wiley, whom I had the privilege of hearing in a revival on my college campus, said that the harps in this passage are symbols of the harmonies of the heavenly life. When we speak of the divine nature as rhythmical, we mean the moral harmonies of God. His nature is so delicately tuned that no discord mars the music. God is purely harmonious in the working of His own being.[2]

God put a song into us, but sin distorted it and garbled it. Sin made personality a disorganized chaos and destroyed the perfect harmony. It brought discord into life. When a person comes into a vital, living relationship with Jesus Christ, the melody that sin had so terribly muted begins to emerge.

Here on earth we are imperfect instruments that continually need adjustment and need to be attuned to the divine harmonies. Though God has restored the song of heaven to the soul of one redeemed, we must still contend with the diabolical disturber of our peace. He aims to thrust discord into our holy lives.

But a holy people respond to a holy God. They strive to perfect "holiness out of reverence for God" (2 Cor. 7:1). They make every effort to "pursue peace with all men, and holiness, without which no one will see the Lord" (Heb. 12:14, NKJV). They endeavor to "keep the unity of the Spirit through the bond of peace" (Eph. 4:3). They may be "partakers of the divine nature" (2 Pet. 1:4, NKJV).

We have seen that God does a masterful work for us in the experiences of conversion and sanctification. He solves the sin problem in our life. But we must remember that we still have our basic humanity. Our infirmities, frailties, weaknesses, and emotional dispositions are not eliminated when we are sanctified.

Inconsistencies or Human Nature?

I know many Christians who have become disillusioned about the experience of heart holiness because they felt it should be the solution to every problem. It is not an automatic answer nor a sure cure for all our defects of mind and soul or faulty judgment. Satan does not die when we are sanctified. We are not always aware of the extent of damage done by the Fall. The physical, social, psychological, and emotional results of sin must still be reckoned with. These effects go far beyond what we suffered morally and spiritually.

Dr. W. T. Purkiser, in referring to what is called "the residual effects of the Fall," said: "The very fabric of our humanity is disturbed, distorted, and damaged. We are but maimed and crippled, disoriented and disorganized copies of the original God planned. The triumph over sin is real and total."[3]

William Cessna reminds us:

> Even a sanctified person has to live with his own life history, with any deprivations he might have had, with the traumatic experiences of his past which continue to remain dynamic with him. There is help for such conditions if one is willing to "work through" such involvements; but to say that these experiences are automatically "cleansed" at sanctification is to do injustice to the doctrine.[4]

Christians must choose to have the discords eliminated from their life or accept the alternative of being discordant souls instead of enjoying a holy harmony.

Sanctified Christians will still experience negative emotions—worry, anxiety, impatience, anger, etc. It is when motives become impure and one stoops to unchristian behavior that emotions will lead to sin. All Christians need the help of the Holy Spirit daily to improve their emotional control and its active expression.

Excessive Anxiety?

If we allow it, the cares and anxieties of this world can starve the supernatural life within. Yet, there is a degree of anxiety that is a natural part of our lives. It is a part of responsible living.

When I was a little girl I studied the violin. It didn't take me long to learn that when I got too much tension in a violin string, it would soon break and I was in trouble. Those four strings were important to me if I was going to make music. I needed to learn to tune my violin correctly. Some anxiety may be basic to the melody of our lives.

We all know people who live with an excessive amount of anxiety. They are indecisive and fearful. They worry about their shortcomings and failures, and they cannot seem to make up their minds about anything. Anxiety becomes a way of life for them and they are tortured by it. Neurotic obsessions and phobias are an enormous concern. Their earthly possessions have robbed them of an inward freedom because they have never learned to empty their heart of useless cares and worries. Serenity and peace seem to be beyond their grasp.

Such excessive daily worry and anxiety cannot be justified in the Christian life. But it is something we need to understand and find help for. Some find reading of Scripture a great source of relief, others look to music to calm the inner spirit, some exercise, and others find good literature to help them in their need. Then let us not forget the importance of commitment of our cares to Him who cares for us. There is open access to the throne of grace.

One morning when I was feeling an enormous amount of stress and was overwhelmed by many things that needed attention, I was reading the classic by Madame Guyon, *Experiencing the Depths of Jesus Christ*. I came across the following lines that I recorded in my journal and have referred to many times since. She wrote:

> Child—you always take life too seriously—with too heavy a spirit, too anxious a mien. A true child of mine has no need to worry so. You act as if you think you have to do everything yourself, as if I, your Burden Bearer, am not with you at all. Satan is the one who wants you burdened down, fatigued, feeling overwhelmed with work.[5]

The beautiful words by John Greenleaf Whittier deserve to be sung often in this day of stressful living:

> *Drop Thy still dews of quietness*
> *Till all our strivings cease.*
> *Take from our souls the strain and stress,*
> *And let our ordered lives confess*
> *The beauty of Thy peace.*

Out of Harmony with Negative Attitudes

I once knew a Christian lady with a very negative, pessimistic attitude. To be around her made everyone miserable. She had developed the habit of looking for sin and sickness in everyone. Her tongue was full of sharp criticism. I never heard her give a compliment or affirm anyone. She rarely smiled. Her attitude reminded me of the words by psychologist William James, "The attitude of unhappiness is not only painful, it is also mean and ugly."[6]

Attitudes are learned from others or from the home. How important for Christians to examine their attitudes frequently and strive to develop wholesome attitudes that bring glory to God. John Homer Miller wrote: "Your living is determined not so much by what life brings to you as by the attitude you bring to life; not so much by what happens to you as by the way your mind looks at what happens. Circumstances and situations do color life, but you have been given the mind to choose what the color should be."[7]

Dissonant Relationships

Perhaps the most surprising aspect of holiness to many Christians is in the area of interpersonal relationships. They are shocked with the discovery that perfect love is not always conveyed by a person's outward personality. In human relationships there is not always successful functioning of every part of the Body of Christ with every other part.

There can be unpleasant misunderstandings that cause concern about another's sanctified experience. We should realize there are many factors that affect the way people react to situations and view problems. There is within the church a great variety of personalities. Some people are abrasive and tactless, there are opinionated individuals, different temperaments, cultural variations, and those who are emotionally immature. In even the closest relationships, tensions and misunderstandings will occur. But conflict, discord, and lack of harmony among Christians should not persist very long without remedying the situation and allowing the peace of God to pass all understanding and misunderstanding.

When professing Christians hurl cutting, insulting, unkind words at one another, their love dissipates to "a resounding gong or a clanging cymbal" (1 Cor. 13:1) in competition with the sweet harmonies of peace and unity. Some have become ineffective in their Christian lives because they have allowed themselves to become a seething cauldron of agitated emotions.

There are Christians that have carried an unforgiving spirit against a brother or sister year after year—not speaking to each other and sitting on opposite sides of the church. The deep resentment becomes not only a hindrance in their own spiritual life but affects their physical body as well, to say nothing of the fact that it becomes a hindrance to revival in the church.

Earnest Christians who are serious about a life that is pleasing to God will not allow Satan to take a stronghold in their life. If they have been filled with the Spirit and sanctified wholly, they will strive toward Christlikeness. They will pray much for the Lord to polish the exterior of their personality and eliminate those faults that are a hindrance to their witness and to the church. They will have a teachable spirit and seek daily to obey the inner checks of God's Spirit.

In his book *Freshness of the Spirit,* Sherwood Wirt describes how the infilling of the Holy Spirit helped eliminate the discords in his attitudes and personality. Wirt wrote:

> A warm feeling spread through me, making me want to lift my voice in praise of the name of Jesus all the time. Much to my surprise, I no longer held any bitterness toward anyone . . . my home situation improved . . . daily depressions that had affected me for years, making me want to drop suddenly in my tracks and say, "I give up," disappeared. No longer did the negative feelings come and go; they went. The world

around me, . . . seemed no longer my battlefield, but rather a part of life to be loved. . . . Goal setting, ambition, promotion, had all been called in for retooling. My thinking was routed into a new channel. In spite of myself I kept smiling and felt silly doing it, but love and happiness had filled my cup, and I couldn't help it.[8]

God the Holy Spirit cleanses our hearts from all sin in response to our faith. He keeps us clean and keeps us from sin as we walk in the light. We must differentiate, however, between our human nature or infirmities and sin. We will struggle and have to work on the maturing of our human nature until the resurrection. God has a majestic harmony for us in the Spirit-filled life. It is a life of victory maintained moment by moment as we walk in obedience and faith. He takes away the inner strain and brings to our life a spiritual wholeness.

> *Thou canst fill me, gracious Spirit,*
> *Though I cannot tell Thee how;*
> *But I need Thee, greatly need Thee;*
> *Come, O come and fill me now.*
> *I am weakness, full of weakness;*
> *At Thy sacred feet I bow.*
> *Blest, divine, eternal Spirit,*
> *Fill with love, and fill me now.*
> —Elwood H. Stokes

10

Songs in the Night Seasons

Life is a precarious journey. We travel down different roads of circumstances and experiences. No two roads are identical. Some take us down paths where we are besieged with complexities. We are battered with problems, difficulties, temptations, and disappointments. Other roads through life are filled with exciting adventures.

Some days we are appallingly conscious of our weaknesses, failures, and deficiencies. Taunting voices make us wonder if we are adequately equipped for the strange pilgrimage. They question us: "Do you have adequate resources for the big stress?" "How will you survive in a crisis you have never met before?" "Will you have enough faith to meet the test of life?" "What will happen when circumstances crash in on you?"

When we are faced with such questions, the Word of God reminds us that the saints of old were not immune from these moods. We see them denying the goodness of God, desperate, doubting, suffering, failing. There were Jeremiah, Job, Habakkuk, Elijah, Peter, Paul, and thousands of God's people through the centuries. They needed reinforcements. They called for strength, hope, and faith. And then, at the moment of despair or imminent collapse, a sudden shaft of light penetrated the darkness to reveal that the Master had been there all the time. He has promised to be with us even unto the end of the world.

Meeting the Inevitable Crisis

The dramatic story of Paganini, the great violinist, has always been an inspiration to me. He was one of the most versatile musicians of all time. We are told that he was a tall, awkward, ungainly person who looked like a scarecrow. When he walked onstage to give a concert, people actually laughed thinking it was a joke. But not for long, for when he played his violin it was veritably a part of him. His violin laughed and sang. It pleaded and cried and thundered and wailed, until people were almost beside themselves with enthusiasm. They refused to leave the concert halls, wanting to hear more. Once in Leghorn, Italy, the following incident took place:

> He shuffled awkward on the stage, the while
> Across the waiting audience swept a smile.
> With awkward stroke when first he drew the bow.
> He snapped a string. The audience tittered low.
> Another stroke. Off flies another string.
> With laughter now the waiting galleries ring.
> A third string breaks its quivering strands,
> And hisses greet the player as he stands.
> He stands, the while his genius unbereft
> Is calm; one string and Paganini left.
> He plays—that one string's daring notes uprise
> Against the storm as though it sought the skies.
> A silence falls. The people bow,
> And those who 'erst had hissed are weeping now.
> And as the last notes quivering died away
> Some shouted "Bravo!" Some had learned to pray.[1]
> —AUTHOR UNKNOWN

Wesley Hager said: "Life is constantly challenging us to make music out of the one string that is left, to make the most out of what we have, to make something beautiful out of the circumstances life has given us. The great glory of life lies in the fact that, whatever those circumstances are, God gives us the power and the spirit to conquer them."[2]

There will be times in our lives when all of us will meet the inevitable crisis. There will be heartaches, unfair criticisms, unkind words, betrayals by trusted friends, discouragements, tragedies, and sorrows. Such experiences are as much a part of the journey as our sun-filled paths of life. The storms, trials, and stresses may be just the tools the Master is using to shape our character into a winsome, useful piece of His workmanship. It will be up to us, however, to search for an oasis of serenity in the desert and discover that His presence is everywhere.

Some people will look for help outside the mainstream of His grace. Some listen to false, God-denying philosophies. There will be those who become aware of certain voices offering diverse counsel. They'll hear them say: "All you have to do is bring into action your own latent reserves of power. You possess undeveloped physical and psychic energies." But the Word of God gives us something better. We do not have to look to our own natural resources. He says: "My grace is sufficient for you. My strength is made perfect in weakness." When we go through the difficult journey of life, there is nothing we ought to pray for more fervently than an acute awareness of the presence of the Living Christ.

Many of the greatest Christian hymns and songs came out of the deep wells of adversity, tragedy, or suffering. The hymn writer George Matheson was a brilliant, young ministerial student of 18. He lost his eyesight almost completely. Eventually he had to give up his research and scholarship in the field of apologetic theology. He had great talent in this field and dearly loved his studies.

Matheson then gave his time and strength to preaching and writing as a minister. It is said that he had a profound influence on all who heard him preach, including Queen Victoria. Through his writings many lives have been transformed by its truths. Matheson could read the hearts of men and women though he was physically sightless. He could also see God in a way that few are able to do.[3] One of my favorite songs that he wrote is "O Love That Wilt Not Let Me Go." The second and third stanzas are significant to those who are hurting:

O Joy that seekest me through pain,
I cannot close my heart to Thee.
I trace the rainbow through the rain,
And feel the promise is not vain
That morn shall tearless be.

O Cross that liftest up my head,
I dare not ask to fly from Thee.
I lay in dust life's glory dead,
And from the ground there blossoms red
Life that shall endless be.

—George Matheson

It is inspiring to know that when events and circumstances turn dark and grim and somber, there is a pitch unheard apart from the mind of Christ by which we can tune our souls.

Beethoven wrote his joyful Second Symphony, the D Major, during a most difficult winter. He was surrounded by shattered hopes and plans that had been thwarted. There was illness, disappointment, and heartache. His deafness was increasing, he was a victim of colic, and the woman who had won his heart and that he dearly loved married another man. Still despite the oppressing circumstances he wrote the joyous music—music that lifts our spirit. In fact, it lifts human hearts wherever it is played.

The resources of God are always greater than the world knows. Even when we face the most difficult circumstance and life seems to go to pieces, God's resources are sufficient.

The Swan Song of Life

A story is told of Socrates when he was approaching the hour of his death. The sentence that was executed against this pagan philosopher was to drink the fatal hemlock. His friends who were about him were weeping. Socrates turned to them and said, "The swan as it sees its end approaching begins its most melodious song, and floating down the river charmed by its own music, meets death with dignity and composure. Man should die with as much cheerfulness as the birds."

"But," said one of his disciples, "death is a terror to us. It unmans us and fills us with dreadful fears. We cannot die like that. We have no swan song with which to float down the river of life in the boundless sea of eternity."

"Go then," replied Socrates, "travel through all lands, spare no toil, no expense, that you may find the song which can charm away the fear of death."

But the pagan world could not catch one swift note of that song from its philosophies. There was nothing in its art, its poetry, or its religion that would give them the hope that Paul has given to us:[4] "'Where, O death, is your victory? Where, O death, is your sting?' The sting of death is sin, and the power of sin is the law. But thanks be unto God! He gives us the victory through our Lord Jesus Christ" (1 Cor. 15:55-56).

Paul could write of death in a major key. He could approach his own death with his sunset anthem: "The time has come for my departure. I have fought the good fight, I have finished the race, I have kept the faith. Now there is in store for me the crown of righteousness, which the Lord, the righteous Judge, will award to me on that day—and not only to me, but also to all who have longed for his appearing" (2 Tim. 4:6-8).

The phrase, "but also to all who have longed for his appearing," is special for us. That puts everyone who has been washed in the blood of the Lamb in line for a triumphant dying. Death is "the last enemy." Death has been shattered by the glory of Christ's resurrection. We need not lose heart in the dark hour. Jesus himself went through the darkest hour of all. He was nailed to a cross, the ugliest symbol of shame that was known. He suffered and died, but as He laid hands on it, He shaped the Cross into such a thing of beauty, power, and triumph for us. When our turn comes, Christ has promised to be there. He tells us there is absolutely nothing to fear. Someone said, "The darkest road with Christ is better than the brightest road without Him." And as Clement of Alexandria remarked, "Christ turns all our sunsets into dawns."[5]

Joyce Kilmer wrote:

> *Because the road was steep and long*
> *And through a dark and lonely land,*
> *God set upon my lips a song*
> *And put a lantern in my hand.*[6]

Before our life closes, we will have to go through sorrow, if we haven't already. It is an experience we cannot escape, for it is a universal experience that comes to all people. Our Lord himself was called "A man of sorrows and acquainted with grief." Sorrow is an agony of spirit; it is the burden on the heart; the pain in the mind; the feeling of "aloneness" when life goes all to pieces. "Sorrow robs life of its radiance and dims the lustre of our days." But Christians have the Comforter, the Holy Spirit, to walk with them and sustain them in the hour of sorrow.

"We conquer sorrow," said Wesley Hager, "when we know we can trust God. Out of the experiences of many, we learn it is often in the dark that God can get closest to us. Only at night can we see the stars."[7]

James S. Stewart wrote:

> The revelation of God in Christ has given us the feel of a divine Hand upon our life—the healing power of the dimension of eternity, the reassuring music of the promise "I will not leave you comfortless, I will come to you." This is not dead dogma I am telling you: it is life transforming truth, verifiable by anyone today. This is the comfort of the Lord.[8]

> *Some thro' the waters, some thro' the flood,*
> *Some thro' the fire, but all thro' the Blood.*
> *Some thro' great sorrow, but God gives a song*
> *In the night season and all the day long.*
> —G. A. YOUNG

PART FOUR

Postlude

11

A Song for All Seasons

It is an old story—music has a certain power. It can drive us to love, to hate, to war, or to God. There are times when it does not drive at all. Instead it lays hands on a troubled spirit—to comfort, to soothe, to heal. Through the years the word *music* has been synonymous with sweetness or joy or beauty. Shakespeare once wrote critically of "the man that hath no music in his soul."

There are times when music speaks to us and we want to reply. There are other times when it makes our hearts leap eagerly. When someone asked Haydn why his music seemed always to be joyous, he replied, "When I think of God, my heart is so full of joy that the notes leap and dance as they leave my pen." There are days when music is like a friend— or a confidante. In short, it is an integral part of living.

Most great music was written according to definite architectural lines. Each small detail has its place, from the first sound to the last. A friend of mine who is an accomplished musician saw a beautiful piece of needlework in a craft shop. It was a cross-stitch pattern with a music score about it. It caught her eye and she purchased it. The music score extended around the margin with the words to the hymn "Immanuel." Inside the pattern were the words: "Music is a fair and glorious gift of God."

When my friend began to cross-stitch the pattern, her well-trained eyes for music detected that something was wrong. As she studied the score she noted that the words, the timing, the notes, and the syllables did not harmonize. They were incorrectly inscribed on the pattern. My friend, of course, was not pleased with the distortion of the harmony. Because she liked the pattern very much, she was determined to correct the work. After four hours of meticulous work on graph paper she had made every detail minutely accurate. Most people would never have noticed the discrepancy, but she could not live with the disharmony.

This book reflects upon the music and song that will come to us from the harmony in our inner life. We *can* experience joy and peace, a sense of direction and destiny. The secret is to focus on a positive, disciplined life in the Spirit and the importance of allowing Christ—our Master Musician—to eliminate the discords and tune with precision our imperfect instruments.

In the discipline of our lives we must learn the wisdom of seizing the moments to draw apart to listen to Christ whisper to our hearts those unseen and eternal truths. Such times can be a source of power that will produce the music in our soul.

Johann Sebastian Bach was the father of a large family. He was often interrupted to rock a fretful baby or to give a piece of bread to a hungry person. At night, however, when everyone was in bed and the world was still, Bach would walk out into the night alone under the stars and the shadow of the trees. There in the stillness he sensed the grandeur, beauty, and order of the universe and communed with his Lord. Today as we hear the divine, immortal harmonies he wrote, our hearts are blessed.

When we learn to live in Christ's presence we will not try to manage our days as though He were far from us. He is able to make a difference in the events we have to encounter in our day. He promises to come into every experience with His grace and power and give to us the serenity and courage that we need to communicate His love to others.

Several years ago as I read Ann Morrow Lindbergh's little book, *Gift from the Sea,* I wrote in my journal her concept of "inner harmony." The words are often quoted by other writers, but they are still relevant for us. She wrote:

> I want first of all . . . to be at peace with myself. I want a singleness of eye, a purity of intention, a central core to my life that will enable me to carry out these obligations and activities as well as I can. I want, in fact—to borrow from the language of the saints—to live "in grace" as much of the time as possible . . . By grace I mean an inner harmony, essentially spiritual, which can be translated into outward harmony.[1]

The song will come spontaneously if there is inner harmony—a song for every season of our life. Great is God's faithfulness. Every sunset is followed by a sunrise. Every winter is followed by summer. If we plant seeds, we can expect a harvest. The sun and the moon and the planets have their definite orbits. There are innumerable stars moving in patterns. They can be charted by astronomers thousands of years in advance. And best of all, God fulfills His pledge to His people—"Morning by morning new mercies we see."

Let us "sing to the Lord as long as we live."

Let us "praise God to our last breath!"

Notes

Preface

1. Wesley H. Hager, *Mastering Life with the Master* (Grand Rapids: William B. Eerdmans Publishing Co., 1966), 44.

Chapter 1—Hearing the Music

1. Henri Nouwen, *Seeds of Hope*, ed. Robert Durback (Toronto: Bantam Books, 1989), 22.
2. Ronald Allen and Gordon Borror, *Worship: Rediscovering the Missing Jewel*, cited in Angela E. Hunt, "Managing the Music in Your Home," *Herald of Holiness*, May 1991, 4.

Chapter 3—The Melody of Love

1. Richard S. Taylor, *Life in the Spirit* (Kansas City: Beacon Hill Press of Kansas City, 1966), 51, 52.
2. C. S. Lewis, *Beyond Personality* (London: Bles, 1944), 63.
3. Ibid., 64.

Chapter 4—A Symphony of Truth

1. A. W. Tozer, *Root of the Righteous* (Harrisburg Pa.: Christian Publications, 1955), 10, 11.
2. Charles Colson, *Who Speaks for God?* (Westchester, Ill.: Crossway Books, 1985), 95.
3. Frank Laubach, *Letters by a Modern Mystic* (Westwood, N.J.: Fleming H. Revell Co., 1937), 12.
4. E. Stanley Jones, *Abundant Living* (Nashville: Abingdon Press, 1942), 58.
5. Tozer, *Root of the Righteous*, 11.
6. Ibid., 12.
7. Jones, *Abundant Living*, 58.
8. Dick Winn, *Ministry*, January 1986 (Silver Spring, Md.: International Journal for Clergy), 4.
9. *Through the Years with Wesley, An Anthology*, comp. and ed. Frederick C. Gill (Nashville: Upper Room, 1983), 9.
10. Nicholas Herman of Lorraine (Brother Lawrence), *The Practice of the Presence of God* (New York: Fleming H. Revell Co., 1895), 34.
11. J. Paul Turner, *The Music of Pentecost* (Winona Lake, Ind.: Light and Life Press, 1951), 58.

Chapter 5—Tuned to the Holy Spirit

1. James S. Stewart, *The Wind of the Spirit* (Nashville: Abingdon Press, 1968), 97.
2. A. W. Tozer, *Knowledge of the Holy* (New York: Harper and Row, Publishers, 1961), 9.
3. Richard Foster, *Celebration of Discipline* (San Francisco: Harper and Row Publishers, 1978), 2.
4. Jones, *Abundant Living*, 53.
5. Amy Carmichael, "Tune Thou My Harp" (London: Society of Promoting Christian Knowledge), cited by Bertha Munro, *The Years Teach* (Kansas City: Beacon Hill of Kansas City, 1970), 332.
6. William Barclay, *Matthew, Vol. 1* (Philadelphia: Westminster Press, 1975), 350.

7. Barclay, *Letter to Ephesians and Galatians* (Philadelphia: Westminster Press, 1976), 14.
8. Thomas á Kempis, *Imitation of Christ,* a new translation by Betty I. Knott (Cleveland: Collins-Fontana Books, 1963), 65.
9. Andrew Murray, *With Christ in the School of Prayer* (Westwood, N.J.: Fleming H. Revell Company, 1952), 32.
10. Dietrich Bonhoeffer, *Letters and Papers from Prison* (New York: Macmillan Publishing Co., 1953), 102.
11. Jones, *Abundant Living,* 53.
12. Thomas Kelly, *A Testament of Devotion* (New York and London: Harper and Brothers Publishers, 1941), 35.
13. Mary Martin, "The Healing of Solitude," in *The Guideposts Treasury of Faith* (Carmel, N.Y.: Guideposts Associates, 1970), 124.
14. Thomas Merton, *Life and Holiness* (Montreal, Que.: Herder and Herder, Palm Publishers, 1963), 10.

Chapter 6—Forming a Biblical Score

1. Charles Colson, *Who Speaks for God?* (Westchester, Ill.: Crossway Books, 1985), 88.
2. Francis Schaeffer, *He Is There and He Is Not Silent* (Wheaton, Ill.: Tyndale House Publishers, 1972), 78.
3. Charles Colson, *Kingdoms in Conflict* (New York: William Morrow and Co.; Grand Rapids: Zondervan Publishing House, 1987), 224.
4. Steve Harper, *Devotional Life in the Wesleyan Tradition* (Nashville: Upper Room, 1983), 30.
5. Spurgeon quote, cited by Chuck Swindoll, *Strengthening Your Grip* (Waco, Tex.: Word Books, 1982), 20.
6. James S. Stewart, *Wind of the Spirit,* 109.
7. Thomas Merton, *Thoughts in Solitude,* cited by Bob Benson, Michael W. Benson, *Disciplines for the Inner Life* (Waco, Tex.: Word Books, 1985), 81.
8. Tozer, *Root of the Righteous,* 93.
9. Foster, *Celebration of Discipline,* 3.
10. Jones, *Abundant Living,* 53.
11. Laubach, *Letters by a Modern Mystic,* 16.
12. Ruth Vaughn, *Write to Discover Yourself* (Garden City, N.Y: Doubleday Co., 1980), 14.
13. Susan Annette Muto, *Pathways of Spiritual Living,* cited by Benson, *Disciplines for the Inner Life,* 99.

Chapter 7—Joy—the Crescendo of Inner Harmony

1. Norman Vincent Peale, *Treasury of Joy and Enthusiasm* (Pawling, N.Y: Foundation for Christian Living, 1960), 80.
2. E. Stanley Jones, *Growing Spiritually* (New York: Abingdon Press, 1968), 140.
3. Ibid.
4. Watchman Nee, *The Joyful Heart, Daily Meditations* (Wheaton, Ill.: Tyndale House Publishers, 1978), meditation for April 22, 1972.
5. Quoted in Peale, *Treasury of Joy,* 35.
6. Ibid., 169.
7. *Letters of C. S. Lewis* (San Diego: Harcourt Brace Jovanovich, 1958), 179.
8. W. Phillip Keller, *The High Cost of Holiness* (Eugene, Oreg.: Harvest House Publishers, 1988), 78.

9. C. S. Lewis, *The Great Divorce* (New York: Macmillan Publishing Co., 1946), 72.

Chapter 8—Sounds of Praise and Worship

1. Donald P. Hustad, "Let's Not Just Praise the Lord," *Christianity Today,* November 6, 1987, 30.
2. C. S. Lewis, *The Joyful Christian* (New York: Macmillan Publishing Co., 1977), 11.
3. Madame Jeanne Guyon, *Experiencing the Depths of Jesus Christ* (Gardiner, Maine: Christian Books Publishing House, 1975), 102.

Chapter 9—Eliminating the Discords

1. Richard S. Taylor, *A Return to Christian Culture* (Kansas City: Beacon Hill Press of Kansas City, 1973), 87.
2. H. Orton Wiley, *The Harps of God* (Kansas City: Beacon Hill Press of Kansas City, 1971), 13.
3. W. T. Purkiser, *These Earthen Vessels* (Kansas City: Beacon Hill Press of Kansas City, 1985), 57.
4. Ibid.
5. Guyon, *Experiencing the Depths,* 160.
6. Peale, *Treasury of Joy,* 105.
7. John Homer Miller, quoted by Peale, *Treasury of Joy,* 111.
8. Sherwood Eliot Wirt, *Freshness of the Spirit* (San Francisco: Harper and Row Publishers, 1978), 53.

Chapter 10—Songs in the Night Seasons

1. Hager, *Mastering Life with the Master,* 19.
2. Ibid.
3. Don Hustad, "George Matheson," in Billy Graham Team, *Crusader Hymns and Hymn Stories* (Minneapolis: The Billy Graham Evangelistic Association, 1967), 38.
4. Turner, *Music of Pentecost,* 107.
5. Stewart, *Wind of the Spirit,* 102.
6. Hager, *Mastering Life with the Master,* 59.
7. Ibid.
8. Stewart, *Wind of the Spirit,* 152.

Chapter 11—A Song for All Seasons

1. Ann Morrow Lindbergh, *Gift from the Sea* (New York: Pantheon, 1955), 23.